THERE'S MORE
"please pa

Dinner Talk

—365—
ENGAGING CONVERSATION STARTERS
to help you and your family connect

Emily Hall, Philip S. Hall, PhD, *and* Nancy D. Hall, EdD

THERE'S MORE TO SAY THAN JUST
"please pass the salt..."

Dinner
Talk

365
ENGAGING CONVERSATION STARTERS
to help you and your family connect

Emily Hall, Philip S. Hall, PhD, *and* Nancy D. Hall, EdD

Adamsmedia
Avon, Massachusetts

To my parents for encouraging me to keep asking questions.
And to my mentors and friends who enriched my life with their answers.

Published by
Adams Media, a division of F+W Media, Inc.
57 Littlefield Street, Avon, MA 02322. U.S.A.
www.adamsmedia.com

ISBN 10: 1-60550-061-5
ISBN 13: 978-1-60550-061-4
E-ISBN10: 1-4405-0724-4
E-ISBN 13: 978-1-4405-0724-3

Printed in the United States of America.

10 9 8 7 6 5 4 3 2 1

Library of Congress Cataloging-in-Publication Data
is available from the publisher.

This publication is designed to provide accurate and authoritative information with regard to the subject matter covered. It is sold with the understanding that the publisher is not engaged in rendering legal, accounting, or other professional advice. If legal advice or other expert assistance is required, the services of a competent professional person should be sought.

—From a *Declaration of Principles* jointly adopted by a Committee of the American Bar Association and a Committee of Publishers and Associations

Many of the designations used by manufacturers and sellers to distinguish their product are claimed as trademarks. Where those designations appear in this book and Adams Media was aware of a trademark claim, the designations have been printed with initial capital letters.

This book is available at quantity discounts for bulk purchases.
For information, please call 1-800-289-0963.

PREFACE

Some of my most vivid recollections from my childhood are about our family conversations. I was lucky enough to grow up in a household where my parents thought (or at least pretended) that my ideas, my perspectives on things, and my solutions to problems were worth listening to. We talked about ideas or pondered questions at the dinner table and my six-year-old opinion and ideas were valid. If I ever had a dumb idea (and I am certain that I did), my parents never pointed it out to me; I was never told that my answers were wrong. As a result, I thought that I was somebody from an early age.

This book has 365 conversation starters that do not have right—or wrong—answers. Initially, it might be hard for you to facilitate discussions that do not have right answers; adults live in a challenging world where "getting it right" has survival value. Right answers are necessary to graduate from high school. Right answers are necessary to get college degrees. Right answers on job applications are necessary for employment. Right answers are necessary in the workplace to get promoted and earn more money. No wonder we come to place so much importance on right answers. But when it comes to binding the family together, being right is overrated. What is important is to value and affirm family members. If you can do this, you will soon have the family talking and listening to each other. Your children will look forward to coming to the dinner table because it is a special time when they can share their ideas, explore their creativity, and bask in the glow of your approval.

The conversation starters in this book are also designed to help your family members celebrate each other as unique individuals rather than focusing on their traditional family roles; i.e. parent, child, oldest, or youngest. This will require both humility and honesty from the adults at the dinner table. If you expect children to give honest, interesting answers, then the same is required of you. Let me share a personal example to make the point.

My mother was an elementary school principal. Our organized home was evidence of her skill set. However, my disdain for my scheduled bedtime challenged even her. In order to entice me into my bed, she implemented what I came to call our mother-daughter talk time. Every evening she would ask me questions about my day: What made me sad today? What exciting thing happened today? After my surface-level answers, she told me about her day. Since the line between being strong-willed and being defiant is thin, this evening ritual went on for years. During one of our bedtime chats, she told me a most interesting story. When she was eight years old, my age at the time, her brother went into her closet and cut the bows off all of her dresses. The story became my favorite. I asked to hear it again and again. After each retelling I had new questions: Were you mad at your brother? What did you do to get even with him? What did your parents do? The story built a bridge between us—a common understanding of what it was like to be eight years old and to be sad and angry. My goal is to help you build similar bridges with your children. It is my hope that the following conversation starters will engage everyone in laughter, fun, and lively dinner talk.

~Emily Hall

INTRODUCTION
WHY EAT TOGETHER?

The word is out, and you've probably heard it. Children benefit when their families routinely eat together. Why is this? Let's take a look at the ways.

EAT IT UP

Researchers at Harvard Medical School found that when families eat together, the children in the family are fifteen percent less likely to be overweight. That makes sense. When families don't sit down together at the dinner table, children often fill up by snacking on high-calorie junk food. However, when everyone in the family gathers at the dinner table, children have been observed eating such strange and wonderful things as lettuce, apples, meat, and bread—all nutritious foods with lots of vitamins and protein. Researchers at the University of Illinois studied the eating habits of students in grades four to six who regularly ate dinners with their families and compared their diets to those of similar-aged students who did not. They found that the students who ate family dinners consumed more vegetables, more fruit and juice, and less sugar-laced soda.

HEAD TO THE TOP OF THE CLASS

Would you believe that when family members eat dinner together their children get better grades? Well, it's true! Researchers at the University of Illinois sampled a large group of children aged seven to eleven and divided them into two groups. One group of children regularly ate dinner with their families and the other group of children seldom ate dinner with their families. The researchers found that the children who regularly ate dinner with their families got better grades and also scored higher on those important end-of-year achievement tests.

A study by Louis Harris and Associates provided further confirmation of this link. They surveyed 2,000 high school seniors by measuring the students' academic skills and asking them a variety of lifestyle questions. The researchers concluded that students who had family dinners four or more times a week had stronger academic skills than the students who had family dinners three or fewer times a week. They also discovered that family dinners were associated with stronger academic skills, regardless of whether the child was from a one-parent or two-parent family.

KEEP IT IN CONTEXT

Families who routinely eat together raise preschool children who have larger vocabularies and better language skills than the preschool children of families who do not regularly eat together. When preschoolers join the family for dinner, they are exposed to big words and complex language structures. Their young brains are wired to try to make sense of what they are hearing. From context and repetition, preschoolers sitting at the dinner table learn the meaning of the big words, and they discover the rules governing the construction of complex language.

LEARN TO ADJUST

This benefit may surprise you. When families eat together regularly, children are better behaved and better adjusted. Researchers at Harvard University followed sixty-five children over eight years to determine which activities contributed the most to healthy child development. They carefully measured the amount of time parents spent playing with their children, reading to their children, encouraging their children to participate in family events, and eating with their children at the dinner table. By now, you can guess what the researchers found! They determined that the factor most strongly associated with well-adjusted children was eating together as a family.

Blake S. Bowden and Jennifer Zeisz, two psychologists at the Children's National Medical Center, surveyed 527 teenagers and divided them into two groups—those who were well adjusted and those who were not well adjusted. Those teenagers who were well adjusted ate dinner with their families an average of 5.4 days a week. In contrast, those teenagers with adjustment problems ate dinner with their families an average of 3.3 days a week. The well-adjusted teenagers in this study were less likely to do drugs or to be depressed. They were more motivated at school. They had healthier and stronger peer relationships and higher self-esteem. Most important, they showed more resilience in the face of adversity.

TALK IT OUT

In the 1990s, Oprah Winfrey sponsored a Family Dinner Experiment. Working with five families, she persuaded the members of each family to eat together every night for a month. To give the experiment a chance of working, Oprah asked the families to commit to staying at the dinner table for a half hour each evening. As part of the experiment, everyone in each of the five families kept a journal, writing down his or her feelings about the experience of eating together.

The journal entries revealed that most members of each family initially found eating together to be unpleasant, almost stressful. For the first week, the family members did not look forward to having to sit down together at dinner. One long minute at the dinner table dragged to the next. There was a lot of silence and little eye contact. Mostly they just ate. But due to their commitment to Oprah, they kept their promise to eat together as a family every evening. Out of sheer boredom, the members of each family gradually started talking to each other. At first, not a whole lot was said. But a sentence here and a remark there gradually evolved into conversations. Sometime during the month, something just short of a miracle happened within each family.

The family members started to look forward to coming together for dinner. They wanted to hear how everyone's day had gone. They wanted to learn what others were planning for tomorrow. In short, the family became connected. When the families came together at the end of the experiment to talk about the experience on the *Oprah Winfrey Show*, the parents were surprised to hear their children talk about how much they came to treasure the time with their parents at the dinner table.

Research studies have found evidence confirming what Oprah Winfrey suspected—that eating as a family leads to better communication. An extensive study by the Center on Addiction and Substance Abuse found that when families started to eat dinner together, even their zip-mouthed teenagers gradually began to participate in the family conversations. The study also found that most teenagers who ate only one or two meals a week with their families secretly wished the family ate more meals together.

It seems that children, even teenagers, like having conversations around the family dinner table. They find out about their family history ("Your grandfather fought in World War II."); they learn about their heritage ("Your grandmother was a German-Russian." "What's a German-Russian?" the teenager asks); and they're allowed to have some input into family functioning ("Would anyone like to see Mt. Rushmore this summer?" "What is Mt. Rushmore?" the six-year-old asks. "Where is it?" the nine-year-old wants to know.). Conversations around the dinner table bring the children into the family, drawing the family together in a supportive, tight-knit group. Conversations around the dinner table give parents a chance to affirm and value their children, giving children a meaningful, functional support system that they will hold onto long after they leave home.

GET GOING

Wow! Seeing all the ways that eating dinner together as a family benefits children, who wouldn't want to get started as soon as possible? Not sure how to get started? The following tips will help you figure it out.

START SMALL

If your family does not routinely eat dinner together, set a goal of getting the family to eat together at least two nights a week. Hold a short family meeting so that everyone can have input into selecting the days of the week and the exact time of the day when everyone can gather around the dinner table. Get everyone to make a firm commitment to being there.

KEEP IT SIMPLE

Don't knock yourself out preparing a gourmet meal. After all, eating is not the main course this particular evening. Even the meal preparer needs to come to the table refreshed and ready to focus his or her energy and attention on the important thing—having a family conversation.

KILL THE MONSTER

Forty percent of families eat dinner with the television blaring in the background. Before everyone sits down to the dinner table, turn off the TV. If the phone rings, let it ring. The caller can phone again or they can leave a voice-mail. If people in the family have cell phones, ask them to push the off button before sitting down to dinner.

It is amazing how many ways we have invented for the world to come between our family members and us. But at dinnertime, family time has to trump all of the world's intrusions.

ENGAGE IN CONVERSATION

To get the promised benefits of eating together, families need to talk to each other. Keep in mind that talking means more than saying "pass the salt" or "eat your peas." Instead, you must actually engage in conversation. As Webster defines it, conversation is the act of talking together. In a conversation, one person talks while other people listen, and then the talker becomes the listener. In a spontaneous, fluid manner, family members share their thoughts, their dreams, their concerns, their ups and downs. They become connected.

But it's not only what you say to each other at the dinner table that matters, it's how you say it. At the dinner table, no one is ever wrong. There is no such thing as a stupid comment. During these dinner table conversations, everyone is emotionally safe. As tempting as it might be, dinner table conversations are not the time or place to give advice, pontificate, lecture, or teach. However, your children will learn. They will learn respect because they see you being respectful. They will learn to be good citizens because they listen to you being one. They will learn to value their family because they are touched when you value them.

HOW IS THIS SET UP?

This book contains 365 conversation starters. Some of the conversation starters allow your children's imaginations to run free (If we dug a hole fifty feet deep in the backyard, what do you think we would find in the bottom of the hole?). Other conversation starters are designed to let your children see that you and the other adults at the table were once kids themselves (What is the dumbest thing you ever did?). A few of the conversation starters are intended to help your children start to think about social responsibility (If you could do one thing to make our town a better place to live, what would it be?). Finally, some conversation starters address the important topic of family members valuing each other (What is one thing about yourself that you think everyone in the family should know?). You can go through the conversation starters in order or you can select one together just before your family sits down at the table. Pick the conversation starter that is most in keeping with your family's mood and needs on that particular evening. If the family seems stressed and listless, a fun conversation starter might be the right choice. If the family recently watched a movie with profound implications and is feeling contemplative, a deeper conversation starter might be appropriate.

The questions you'll find in this book are geared toward kids in elementary school. If you see a question that doesn't seem appropriate for your children, feel free to skip it until they're older or phrase it in a way that you think they'll be able to understand. Really, what matters is that you're talking—and listening—to your child or children. You will also want to use some discretion when it comes to answering questions that call for self-disclosure of things that your children might find upsetting, too adult, or which are just not appropriate. For example, when asked, "What is the dumbest thing you ever did?" you probably would not want to say, "Accepting my current job," before launching into a discussion regarding how much you hate your work.

At the end of the day, it doesn't matter which questions you ask or what conversation starters you choose as long as you spend your mealtime engaged in dinner talk. So, put these tips to use and get talking!

Bon appetit!

DATE: _____ / _____ / _____

❏ *Who is your favorite athlete and what do you like about him or her?*

WHAT TO EXPECT

Your child's favorite athlete does not have to be a professional. Whereas adults tend to like an athlete because they envy their skill at the game and young adolescents are apt to say that their favorite athlete plays for their local high school or elementary school, your young children are apt to like a particular athlete because he "looks cool" in his Nike hat, or she looks happy on commercials. Of course, it is even okay if your preschooler says that Superman is his favorite athlete. After all, isn't leaping over tall buildings in a single bound an athletic event?

Keep the Conversation Going by . . .

Asking your child, "Why is this person your favorite athlete?" and "Is the person also a good role model?" If he doesn't know what a role model is, take the time to explain what you mean. Talk about who you see as a role model and why. Tell your child who you love to watch play and why. Explain whether you admire the person as an athlete or person or both, so your child can understand the difference. Ask your child if she would like to play the same sport as the athlete she talks about. If so, how can she make that happen? Why (or why not) is that athlete a good role model?

2

DATE: _____ / _____ / _____

❑ *Tell us about your two best friends.*

WHAT TO EXPECT

As your children grow older, they spend more time with friends, who influence their view of themselves and others. As the adage says, "Birds of a feather flock together." Your children make their own friends at school and you may not know these friends, unless you make an effort to learn about them. You can learn a lot about your children by finding out about their best friends and what kinds of things they like to do together.

Keep the Conversation Going by . . .

Asking your child to tell you about the last time she saw a certain friend or group of friends. When was this? What happened that last time they were together? Who else was there? What kinds of things does she like to do with her friends? Tell your child a little bit about your own friendships. Talk about the things you and your friends used to do at her age.

DATE: _____ / _____ / _____

❑ *What drives you crazy?*

WHAT TO EXPECT

This is meant to be a light-hearted discussion of pet peeves, not an attack session. However, family members might become aware of things they do that upset another family member, which can be eye-opening. Your children under age seven probably can't identify what drives others crazy, but they can think of some incidents where someone in the family was annoyed with them and this is a beginning awareness. As they mature, they start to acquire the ability to step into another person's shoes. Your children over age ten can often predict what would drive another person crazy and are probably ready and willing to engage in a discussion about what adults and siblings do that drives them crazy! But don't take it personally and don't let your children turn this into a gripe session where they pick each other apart. Keep it light and fun.

Keep the Conversation Going by . . .

Explaining, if it feels right, why adults sometimes do things that drive children crazy. Ask your child if he can come up with a solution to the thing that drives him nuts. Does this thing always drive him crazy, or does it happen on some days more than others? Does this thing drive anyone else crazy?

DATE: _____ / _____ / _____

❏ *If you were an inventor, what would you create?*

WHAT TO EXPECT

Initially, everyone is apt to sit there looking around, try-ing to think of something. Don't panic. Silence seldom does harm. When ideas start flowing, you can expect school-age children to think of neat toys. Teenagers will conjure up vehicles that can do amazing things, like cars that can jump across canyons or go at tremendous speeds. Parents are apt to mention labor-saving devices.

Keep The Conversation Going by . . .

Telling your child what you would invent and why. Then ask him to think of a particular problem that needs a solution or something he wishes he could do but can't. What would he invent to solve that problem? Who would use his invention? How much would he charge for his invention if someone wanted to buy it?

DATE:_____ /_____ /_____

❑ *If you could be any animal, what animal would you be?*

WHAT TO EXPECT

This is a particularly good conversation starter for your younger children. They are familiar with a variety of animals, and they enjoy using their imaginations. The type of animal young children choose often provides insight into their view of themselves. For example, a child who wants to be a grizzly bear may think of herself as strong or may desire strength because she is being picked on or even bullied at school. A child who wants to be a rabbit may like to be held and comforted. A child who wants to be a puppy may be saying that she is friendly and does her best to please. Of course many children may also base their choice on a recent movie or experience that involved animals.

Keep the Conversation Going by . . .

Asking your child why she would want to be that kind of animal. What would she do each day? What would be fun and what would be hard about being that animal? Then, tell her what type of animal you'd like to be and why and ask her how she would feel about having, for example, a parakeet for a mother or a shark for a dad. How would the animals you and you child chose get along with each other?

TAKE A TIP:
GIVE LOTS OF POSITIVE FEEDBACK

Positive feedback is the foundation upon which family members build their ideas of self and their self-esteem. By valuing and praising your children, you show that you are listening with both ears. When you value what your child is saying, you value that child for who he or she is. The importance of this cannot be overstated.

As you value your children and give them positive feedback, they feel free to share important things in their developing lives with you because they know they are emotionally safe. By doing this, you become a safe harbor in times of stress and uncertainty, a sanctuary when respite is needed. One reason for having family dinner conversations is that they provide you with golden opportunities to value and give positive feedback to your children. Here are some positive comments:

- Wow! You have a great idea!
- I didn't know anything about that.
- Thanks for sharing that information.
- That is interesting!

The opposite of a valuing or encouraging comment is a putdown. Try to avoid saying the following to your children:

- I can't believe you said that!
- That's not right.
- That is stupid.

Remember, one putdown has the ability to negate 100 positive comments.

DATE:_____ /_____ /_____

❑ *What is the best thing that happened to you today?*

WHAT TO EXPECT

This conversation starter will get your dinner talk off to a positive start, and will encourage your family to think about what they have to be thankful for. It may take a bit to get your children to offer really insightful stories or thoughts. The best thing that happened that day might have been that the cafeteria had pizza for lunch. As you talk together, this starter will give your children insight into the things you value as a family. Sharing positive stories will strengthen family bonds and reinforce the need for the family dinner. This might even begin a healthy pattern of positive daily reflection.

Keep the Conversation Going by . . .

Encouraging your child to tell you more about the best part of his day. Where did this great thing happen? When did it happen? Why does he think it happened? Make sure you answer these questions too and talk about your own day. If your child can't think of anything to say, ask specific questions about things you know he enjoys and did that day.

DATE: _____ / _____ / _____

❑ *You are giving out a Best Teacher award. Who would you give it to and why?*

WHAT TO EXPECT

Expect each family member to reflect on a teacher who made some kind of difference in his or her life. For your child, a favorite teacher could be someone who made the classroom a fun place to be. It could be a favorite teacher who has touched your child's life in a profound way. Your younger children might describe a teacher who provides them with emotional security in the classroom. For older children, a favorite teacher is often someone who relates well to the students and their culture. Throughout this conversation, children may get an understanding of the importance of doing things that contribute to the greater good.

Keep the Conversation Going by . . .

Asking your child to compare this teacher to other ones she's had. What did this teacher do that set him or her apart? What would the award be? A simple plaque? A bushel of apples? Encourage your child to try to think of a unique award that reflects the reasons she chose this person for the award in the first place. You may also want to ask your child what subject she would like to teach if she decides to become a teacher. Talk about teachers that had a positive impact on your life to whom you would give an award.

8

DATE:_____ /_____ /_____

❑ *If you could build a new animal, what would it be like?*

WHAT TO EXPECT

Your children under the age of eight are likely to create an animal that would be a good companion and source of comfort. Older children will probably create an animal that is weird or scary. You and the other parent would probably create an animal that would be useful, such as an animal that eats dirt and crumbs off the floor. You can expect your kids to use their imaginations when answering this question.

Keep the Conversation Going by . . .

Asking about any special talents your child's animal has. Can it jump high? Can it change colors? What does your child like about the animal he invented? Where would that animal live—in the house, in the forest, or in his bedroom? What would he call the animal?

DATE:_____ /_____ /_____

❑ *Tell us about the first time you talked in front of your class or in front of a bunch of people.*

WHAT TO EXPECT

Most of us are apprehensive about talking in front of people and you should not expect your child to be the exception. In fact, you may want to begin this conversation by telling a story about your experiences with public speaking. Your children will love to hear you talk about how you were apprehensive talking to a large group of people for the first time and will learn that they are emotionally safe in sharing personal feelings with you.

Keep the Conversation Going by . . .

Asking others at the table to give public speaking advice; older siblings may have a lot of advice to give. But as a facilitator, you need to carefully read your child's body language. If the advice is not being appreciated, redirect the conversation and ask your child what she talked about. Did she have butterflies in her stomach before she started to speak? Get everyone at the table to relate their experiences. You could ask everyone to share two stories—one when it was easy and another when public speaking was difficult.

DATE:_____ /_____ /_____

❑ *What do you think a day in the life of a rancher is like?*

WHAT TO EXPECT

In 1953, 43 percent of people in the United States lived on farms or ranches. Today, only 1 percent of us live in the country, and only a very few are ranchers. But you can still expect your children to have an idealized image of a rancher. They may think that a modern-day rancher is the same as a stereotypical cowboy. Perhaps they are certain that he rides his horse across the range, herding and roping cattle. They might talk about chuck wagons and bonfires. You and other adults at the table will know that a rancher's life isn't as glamorous as the kids may make it out to be; a rancher is typically doing day-to-day work, like using a tractor to put up hay or checking their water tanks. But this is a case where being right is over-rated. Simply add your thoughts as to what you think a day in the life of a rancher is like.

Keep the Conversation Going by . . .

Asking your child if he would like to be a rancher. If so, why? If he were a rancher, how far would he want to live from town? What kinds of animals would he like to have on his ranch? What would be the hardest part about being a rancher? The most enjoyable part? Be sure to put in your own two cents about this topic as well.

DATE:_____ /_____ /_____

❑ *What is the one thing that might happen to you tomorrow that would make it a really good day?*

WHAT TO EXPECT

Children will reflect on what makes a good day in their eyes, which might mean things such a long recess, a snow day, a good grade on a test, or a birthday party at school. As they talk, they can start to see that they can do things to make their day better. People who see themselves as steering their own ship generally have better mental health and are happier. As they grow older, it is healthy for your children to shift from feeling that outside things control their feelings and what happens to them to realizing that what *they* do plays a large role in determining what happens to them. You will want to listen (only listen) to where your children are on this continuum of feeling controlled by outside events to feeling a sense of control.

Keep the Conversation Going by . . .

Asking your child where that good thing will happen, if it happens? Why would it make his day good? Is it very likely to happen? You may want to tell him what makes a day good for you and ask how you can make his day even better.

DATE:_____ /_____ /_____

❑ *What was the most boring part of your day?*

WHAT TO EXPECT

Your children often think that they are the only ones who get bored. They will benefit from learning that boredom is a common, universal experience. Expect your children to report that they get bored in school. You may want to ask some questions to determine how much of the school day they are bored and what it is about school that bores them. They might say they find math boring or that doing worksheets is boring. However, don't panic. It is common and completely normal for children to report that they are bored in school. After all, teachers are not entertainers. There simply are times during a typical school day when nearly every student, at one time or another, feels bored.

Keep the Conversation Going by . . .

Asking your child how long he was bored. What was he doing while he was bored? Did he do anything to end the boredom? Take the conversation a step further and ask your child to tell you about the most boring day he can possibly imagine. Be sure that you and the adults at the table answer too, as it is helpful and can be humorous to commiserate about boredom.

DATE: _____ / _____ / _____

❑ *Who is the funniest person you know? What makes that person funny?*

WHAT TO EXPECT

This should be a fun, light-hearted discussion, and everyone should be able to contribute memorable anecdotes. Your young children are likely to talk about something the funny person did that inadvertently made them look foolish. They will probably equate a funny person with a funny incident, like when a kid at school tripped over his shoelace and knocked over a stack of books. Your older children can probably see that "funny" resides within the person. However, they may not distinguish between people who are intentionally funny (such as those who do impressions at the lunch table) and people who consistently but unintentionally do funny things (like a teacher who always calls a few students by the wrong names).

Keep the Conversation Going by . . .

Asking your child where she first met this person. How long has she known him? Does she like this person? Does she think this person tries to be funny and light-hearted? Why does she think that person tries to be funny? When this person is funny, do other people laugh? How does your child think this person feels when he or she makes other people laugh? What does the person do that is funny? Talk about some funny people you've known and things they've done.

DATE:_____ / _____ / _____

❑ *If you could try a new sport, what would that sport be and why would you want to try it?*

WHAT TO EXPECT

There will probably be a pause while everyone thinks about this topic. Sharing your thoughts first should get the conversation rolling. Talk about the sport you would try and why it appeals to you. Discuss whether you think it would be hard to learn. Once people start talking, the question might prompt your child to start thinking about an activity or sport that would broaden and enrich his or her life.

Keep the Conversation Going by . . .

Saying something like, "Oh, I didn't know you were interested in baseball/football/curling." Ask your child if he thinks that he might like to try that sport some-time. Does he know anyone who plays that sport? You may also want to offer to watch a game (in person or on TV) with your child. Ask him if that's something he would be interested in. Ask your child what appeals to him about that sport and offer your own opinions about it as well.

DATE:_____ /_____ /_____

❑ *If you could adopt a single feature from a wild animal, what would it be (e.g. horns from a deer, the ability to run fast like an antelope, or maybe even a poisonous bite like a snake)?*

WHAT TO EXPECT

Expect your children nine and younger to select a feature that they would like to possess, such as being able to run fast or wanting a warm furry coat. They are likely to pick something that sounds cool or weird. Older children might select a feature that connotes power, like long claws. A few whimsical older children are apt to select a feature of shock value, such as big teeth like a wolf.

Keep the Conversation Going by . . .

Having your child tell you why he would like that to have that feature. How does he think his friends would react when they saw him? Would they run away, or would they wish they had that feature too? If your child could assign each member of the family a specific animal trait, what traits would he give to each person? Share which animal features you would like to try out for yourself.

16

DATE:_____ /_____ /_____

❏ *When you were little, what is one thing that you wished you could do but weren't allowed to because you were too young?*

WHAT TO EXPECT

Children will connect with their parents by realizing that they too were once young and not permitted to do some things. Everyone at the table will be able to vividly remember that one thing they weren't allowed to do because they were too young. Even your children who are five or six will clearly be able to describe something they were not allowed to do, but now can do, such as holding the dog's leash, stirring a pot that is cooking, or putting a DVD in to play by themselves.

Keep the Conversation Going by . . .

Asking your child to tell you how she felt when she was not allowed to do that specific thing. Was she frustrated? Angry? Accepting? How old was she when she finally got to do that thing? How did it feel when she first did it? Was it exciting? Was it less of a big deal than she thought it would be? Looking back on it, does your child think it is reasonable that she wasn't able to do that when she was little?

DATE:_____ /_____ /_____

❏ *If you could make a television show about our family, what would it be like?*

WHAT TO EXPECT

Expect your children's answers to closely mirror their favorite television shows. Children eight-years-old and younger who like to watch cartoons on Saturday morning are apt to cast members in that genre. Children in the ten-year-old range may suggest a value-based family show. Older children might suggest a sci-fi show along the lines of *Star Wars* or some kind of a reality-based show.

Keep the Conversation Going by . . .

Having your child tell you more about the show. What role would he assign to each family member? Would your house be the setting for the show, or would your family be somewhere far away? Ask your child to describe an episode. Offer details about the show you would invent and chat about whether it would be fun to appear on the shows everyone has suggested.

DATE: _____ / _____ / _____

❑ *Tell us about the nicest person you know and why you think that person is nice.*

WHAT TO EXPECT

For your children who are six and younger, a nice person might be someone who gives them things or plays with them. If your children are seven to eleven, they are apt to name someone who makes them feel valued and emotionally safe; however, they may have difficulty finding the words to express those feelings and might just say "because he's nice" or "I like her" and be unable to offer a real reason. Your older children are ready to look beyond themselves and consider what people do for others.

Keep the Conversation Going by . . .

Asking your child to define what "nice" means to him. Ask for some examples of what is nice. Does he think he is nice in the same way? If not, would he like to be? Take the time to talk about the qualities you look for in a nice person and tell your child why you think he's one of the nicest people you know.

DATE:_____ /_____ /_____

❑ *What things do you do pretty much the same way and at the same time every day?*

WHAT TO EXPECT

Routines are useful. They help keep us organized, and having a semblance of organization generally makes the day go better. This question should prompt each member of your family to think about useful routines. If you have young children, they may not initially get it. If they have something that could be called a routine (like the steps they go through from getting out of bed in the morning to out the door to school), they probably do not even think of those steps as being a routine. So you will probably have to start this conversation by sharing one or two of your own routines. Be sure to mention how this type of organization helps you.

Keep the Conversation Going by . . .

Asking your child how this routine helps her. Can she remember a time when she did not have this routine (i.e. a time when she slept through her alarm clock or was on vacation)? How did things go then? Does she wish that she didn't have to follow a routine every day? If she didn't, what would she do? Does she think she would have more fun if she didn't follow a routine? Why? You might want to share a story about a day your routine got out of whack and how it affected you.

DATE:_____ /_____ /_____

❑ *We're throwing a party and you're in charge. What theme will the party have and what will everyone do?*

WHAT TO EXPECT

Children of every age love parties. So expect everyone in your family to be excited to talk about the party that they'd like to throw. As the ideas are passed from one family member to the next, the party planning will become increasing more elaborate, innovative, and imaginative. Your younger children may focus on the food, games, and decorations—the tangible aspects of the party. Older children may be interested in talking about who they would invite.

Keep the Conversation Going by . . .

Asking your child who he would invite to his party and why. What kind of food would your child serve at his party? Would he like a big cake? Entertainment? Would his guests come in costumes? If so, what kind? Tell your child whom you would like to invite and what type of party you'd like to throw.

DATE:_____ /_____ /_____

❏ *If I asked you to say something nice to someone else, what would you say and whom would you say it to?*

WHAT TO EXPECT

This question will encourage your children to think about how they impact other people. Moreover, it creates the opportunity for them to begin to realize that they have the capacity to have a positive impact on others' lives. Children younger than eight will need examples of what constitutes a compliment. You can help them by starting the discussion by sharing a compliment you gave to someone; and you can also share a compliment that you received from someone, and tell how receiving that compliment made you feel. Children nine and older know what a compliment is, but they are not in the habit of giving them. They too will benefit from hearing how you went about giving a compliment.

Keep the Conversation Going by . . .

Asking your child why he chose that person to compliment. How does he think that person would respond if he gave him or her a compliment? Would that person be surprised? Thankful? Confused? Who gives your child a lot of compliments? How does receiving compliments make him feel? Ask him if giving someone a compliment is something he might actually do. You could share compliments you have received that meant a lot to you, or talk about compliments you've given to others.

DATE:_____ /_____ /_____

❏ *What can your favorite toy do that you would like to do?*

WHAT TO EXPECT

This question will rev up everyone's imagination. It allows kids to explore what they would like to be able to do in their wildest dreams and some of their answers might be quite extreme or stretch the bounds of reality. If your son cites his superhero action figure and says, "He can fly," don't point out that people cannot actually fly. Instead, nurture his imagination and go along for the ride. Expect your children to have an easier time with this question than the adults at the dinner table. But know that it will be good for the adults to take a few years off of their minds and once again imagine the impossible.

Keep the Conversation Going by . . .

Asking your child why he would like to be able to do whatever it is that his toy can do. For example, if he wants to fly, does he want to be able to see your house from the sky? Does he want to see what a bird looks like up close in the air? What is the closest he could come to actually doing that? What does he think it would be like to actually be able to do it? You may also want to tell your child what your favorite toy was when you were younger and what it could do that you always wanted to experience.

DATE:_____ /_____ /_____

❑ *What do you like best about this time of year?*

WHAT TO EXPECT

This question will prompt members of your family to start thinking about fun activities that they could do, making this a good question to ask when the hum-drums have set in and everyone is feeling listless and lethargic (particularly during seasons that keep them cooped up inside). Your children may mention holidays, foods, weather, activities, sports, sights, sounds, or school or family traditions. You can get the ball rolling by sharing your favorite activities for this time of the year.

Keep the Conversation Going by . . .

Asking your child if there is any special place she likes to go at this time of the year. Does she love going to the pool in the summer? To see holiday lights in the winter? Does she have any special memories about something you once did at this time of the year? Maybe your family went apple picking, to a springtime festival, or ice skating? What is her favorite season?

DATE:_____ /_____ /_____

❑ *What is your happiest memory?*

WHAT TO EXPECT

Your children will take time to reflect on some treasured moment, so expect a few minutes of silence. Most children will talk about a big, unusual event that made an impression, such as a birthday party or a vacation. If your child's favorite memory occurred when he was with people outside of your family, you will want to note that. If this is the case, you might also want to nondefensively ask questions to determine what kinds of things your child did with that nonfamily member that resulted in a favorite memory, and ask yourself whether your family does those things. Children eight and younger will probably choose a time when they got something as their nicest memory. For example, a seven-year-old might say, "My favorite memory was last Christmas when I got a skateboard." An older child might say that a favorite memory was an activity that brought her closer to another person, strengthening their bond.

Keep the Conversation Going by . . .

Asking your child for more information about his memory. At the time this memory was being made, did he know right then that it would be something he'd remember for a long time? How did he feel at the time? You may also want to tell your child your favorite childhood memory and your favorite all-time memory.

DATE:_____ /_____ /_____

❑ *Create a story about what happens when you flush the toilet.*

WHAT TO EXPECT

This question is likely to elicit some silly and imaginative answers. Remember, there aren't any right or wrong answers to these conversation starters. Let your child's imagination run free here. You will hear impossible stories (tales of underground worlds, monsters, or people inside the toilet) with some age appropriate bathroom humor thrown in for good measure. Don't feel compelled to give a lesson about how the sanitation system works or chastise your child for talking about bathroom matters!

Keep the Conversation Going by . . .

Throwing out some crazy, fantastical suggestions of your own. Would your child like to jump in the toilet and go along on its trip? Does she think there are any strange creatures (alligators? mermaids? mutants?) that live down there? Would she meet them on her travels? If you had a theory about the toilet as a child, be sure to share it.

DATE:_____ /_____ /_____

❑ *Let's pretend that we're going to take a ten-day, 500-mile canoe trip down a wilderness river. You won't see anyone during the trip and there is no place to buy anything. But since canoes are small, you can take only three things. What would you take?*

WHAT TO EXPECT:

This question will require each of your children to problem solve and use good critical thinking skills. There should be interplay in the discussion. When one thing is mentioned and agreed upon, it limits the possibilities for something else. Expect that your younger children will not appreciate the gravity of the problem. They might want to take their favorite dolls or a baseball. But hey, it is their trip. Your older children are more likely to realize that this is about survival and will bring along many important basics.

Keep the Conversation Going by . . .

Making sure that your child thinks of all eventualities. What if it rained, would he be able to keep dry? Where would he sleep at night? There are bound to be insects. How is he going to keep the insects from feasting on him? What is he planning to eat during this trip? Where might this trip be? Feel free to allow each person to choose their own three items and then compare them. Would you survive as a family if you pooled everything together?

DATE: _____ / _____ / _____

❑ *What is the weirdest thing you have eaten?*

WHAT TO EXPECT

Your children under eight are unlikely to have eaten very many weird things (at least you hope so!), but they are likely to either think they have or say they have. For example, a five-year-old might say, "I ate worms." This sets the stage for topping the last story told. So when the eight-year-old says, "I once ate ants," simply smile. An adolescent at the dinner table might say, "I once tried chocolate-covered grasshoppers," and maybe he or she did. By the time the conversation gets to you and other adults, whatever weird thing you might have eaten will likely seem pretty bland by comparison.

Keep the Conversation Going by . . .

Having your child tell you more about the weird thing she ate. Where did she eat that? Why did she eat it? What did it taste like? Would she ever eat it again? Why or why not? Give some details about the weird things you've eaten. Remember that some things you've eaten without a thought could seem quite weird to a child, such as squid, venison, or wild truffles.

DATE:_____ /_____ /_____

❑ *Your birthday is now a national holiday! How do you want people to celebrate your special day?*

WHAT TO EXPECT

Your children who are ten years old and younger primarily love and focus on national holidays that benefit them personally and directly. Christmas and Hanukkah rank high on the list because of their focus on gift-giving and kid-friendly stories and traditions. You can expect a multitude of suggestions for ways to celebrate a birthday that is now a national holiday. The first line of thought will likely be about getting and giving gifts. Your child might suggest everyone get the day off from school or sing "Happy Birthday" to her. Your child is going to want the day to be all about things he enjoys. Older kids could talk about using the celebration to unite the community, state, or nation for a larger good.

Keep the Conversation Going by . . .

Asking your child what she might accomplish that would result in having the country recognize her birthday as a national holiday. What will she do to show her appreciation? Will she give a speech, ride in a parade, or sponsor a picnic in the park? Tell your child how you would celebrate your own holiday.

DATE: _____ / _____ / _____

❑ *What would your life be like if you could be invisible?*

WHAT TO EXPECT

Your children probably love to imagine the impossible and this question will stir their imaginations, making it a good way to refocus the family and get everyone involved. Your under-seven children are apt to enjoy the idea of being invisible because it would allow them to get away with things, like taking a cookie any time they wanted. Your children between the ages of seven and ten would probably like to be invisible because they could spy on others. Older children are apt to want to use their invisible powers to listen to their peers or even adults so that they can gain insight into the group's dynamics and might reference Harry Potter's invisibility cloak. Without quite knowing it, children of this age are interested in learning how to fit in better and have more influence over these groups.

Keep the Conversation Going by . . .

Having your child go into more detail about the perks (or the disadvantages) of invisibility. Ask him if he would want to be invisible all the time or just some times? What would he do if he were invisible? Would he feel different than he does now? Would his skin be cold? Would you still be able to touch him even if you couldn't see that he was there? Jump into the discussion with your own ideas about invisibility.

DATE: _____ / _____ / _____

❑ *What kind of creature might live on Mars?*

WHAT TO EXPECT

This question should prompt your children to think creatively and use their imaginations. Expect the unexpected and accept it when you hear it. Remember, there are no wrong answers. Many young children will invent a creature. They might describe a fire-breathing monster that roams the planet at night, eating cows. Hearing that, just smile and ask them to tell you more.

Keep the Conversation Going by . . .

Telling your child some of the myths about Martians and asking for her interpretation of those myths. Martians are typically thought of as "little green men." Would her Martian be green? Would her creature be friendly to people? What would that creature eat? Would it be able to talk to her? You can make up your own Martian to entertain your children during this conversation, or even pretend to be one to get a few laughs.

DATE:_____ /_____ /_____

❑ *If you were a bird living in our neighbor-hood, where would you like to sleep?*

WHAT TO EXPECT

This question should prompt your children to think about animals and their struggles to keep warm and comfortable, and also to survive. Your compassionate child, probably under the age of five, might say, "I would want the bird to sleep in my bed with me." Again, there are no wrong answers. But you might ask such things as, "Do you think your covers would be too heavy for you if you were a bird?" Or, "What time do you think birds wake up in the morning?" If your children are between the ages of six and nine they are likely to say, "In a bird-house." Older children are apt to realize that there are a lot of birds and not many birdhouses. They are likely to give more plausible places where a bird might spend the night.

Keep the Conversation Going by . . .

Asking what kind of bird your child would choose to be. Would she be a big bird or a little bird? Would she be brightly colored or would she tend to blend into her surroundings? Would she get wet when it rained or would she find a place to stay dry? How would she keep herself safe from cats? Offer your own opinions about life as a bird.

DATE:_____ /_____ /_____

❑ *What is one thing that every kid your age should have?*

WHAT TO EXPECT

By asking this question, you will likely gain insight into something your child would like to have and has possibly been wishing for quite some time. You will also gain an understanding of your child's maturity level. With few exceptions, your child will name something material, such as a bicycle, video game system, or a baseball glove. However, your child might say revealing things, such as a brother to play with or a dad who will take him camping or show him how to catch fish.

Keep the Conversation Going by . . .

Asking your child to tell you more about what she wants. If she wants a material item ask her if she thinks many kids her age have one. How would a kid be affected if she did not have that item? If your child wants something a little less tangible, ask him how he could go about getting what he wants. If he wants to go camping, maybe offer to plan a weekend trip or just camp in your backyard.

DATE: _____ / _____ / _____

❑ *What is one thing that you think our family should do more often?*

WHAT TO EXPECT

Expect to learn about family activities that your children particularly value and enjoy. You might also hear some good ideas about different activities the family could do to strengthen the bonds. As the saying goes, "Wisdom comes from the mouths of babes." Your children ages six and under are likely to mention the outcome they would like as opposed to the activity that results in the outcome. For example, they are apt to say, "Have fun." Older children are likely to suggest an activity; the older the child, the more specific they will be about what they want to do.

Keep the Conversation Going by . . .

Having your child describe exactly what it is that he likes about the activity he suggested. For example, does he like being outdoors if he chose hiking? Why does he think your family should do that more often? When was the last time your family did that? What do other families do for fun? Would your child like to try something similar? Is there a new activity he can think up that he would like the family to try together? Feel free to talk about things you would like the family to do more often.

34

DATE:_____/_____/_____

❑ *If a genie gave you the choice between being the strongest person in the world or being the smartest person in the world, which would you pick and why?*

WHAT TO EXPECT

Expect your children to reflect on what is important to them and, by implication, why. Your children under six will probably want to be the strongest person in the world. Strength is something they understand and have experienced. As children become older and have the benefit of spending more time in school, they experience how difficult it can be to learn something new. When you finally tell your child what you would choose, your child will get a chance to listen and learn from your perspective.

Keep the Conversation Going by . . .

Having your child weigh both options. What are the pros to being the strongest person in the world? Would he feel like a superhero? What are the cons to being so strong? Would he pull doors off the hinges when he went to open them or have to do something he didn't want to do because of his strength? Why would being the smartest person in the world be useful? Could your child get really good grades in school or invent something cool? You may want to ask him who would come out victorious if the strongest person in the world had to face off against the smartest. Who would win and why?

DATE: _____ / _____ / _____

☐ *What is the dumbest thing you have ever done?*

WHAT TO EXPECT

Your children need to know that adults do not always do everything right. As part of forming a healthy child-parent relationship, you should open up so your children can see your human side. Since sharing blunders and mistakes can be difficult, you should start this conversation by disclosing a foolish thing that you've done. Your children under six will have a difficult time telling the difference between a dumb thing they did (forgetting to put on underwear) and a dumb thing that happened to them (having ketchup spilled on them by someone else). If they offer up the latter, just accept their contribution to the conversation. Children who are nine and older can usually describe a time when they did something dumb. However, they will be sensitive to any ridiculing, so be careful. Laugh with—not at—them.

Keep the Conversation Going by . . .

Asking your child what happened when she did that dumb thing. Was she embarrassed? Did she think it was funny? Did other people think it was funny? What's the dumbest thing she's ever seen anyone else do? How did she react to that?

DATE:_____ /_____ /_____

❏ *If you could build the ultimate tree house, what would it look like?*

WHAT TO EXPECT

There is something about a tree house that probably appeals to your children. They like the thought of being above it all and of having their own space and place. Most children don't picture adults being in their tree house. They will probably offer details of what will be in the tree house and rules about who is allowed in and who isn't. It will be interesting for you to see whether each child talks about "my" tree house or "our" tree house. That will give you insight into sibling cohesiveness.

Keep the Conversation Going by . . .

Asking your child where the tree house would be built. What would make a good tree for a tree house? How would it be decorated? What would the inside of the tree house look like? What color would it be painted? How would people get up and down? Has your child ever been in a tree house? What did that tree house look like? What did he like about it? What would he like to do up there? Read? Play with friends? Sit and daydream? Have a sleepover? Who would he invite into his tree house? If you had a tree house as a child, share the details.

DATE:_____ /_____ /_____

❑ *If you dug an incredibly deep hole in the ground, what do you think you'd find while you were digging?*

WHAT TO EXPECT

Thinking about what is below the surface of the earth has piqued the imagination and curiosity of people of all ages and cultures. No matter where you live, there is likely evidence of history within the first ten feet of dirt and there is definitely interesting paleontology as you get further down. When asking this conversation starter, pose it first to the youngest children in your family. Knowing little about history and probably nothing about paleontology, they will use their imaginations. Such a child might talk about finding gold, strange worms, or even a lost city. Who knows? Older children might be informed enough to know that they might find historical artifacts or fossils.

Keep the Conversation Going by . . .

Keeping your child's imagination going. What would she find when she dug the last few feet of the hole? A popular myth is that you can dig your way to China. Does your child think she can dig her way through to the other side of the earth? If so, what would she do when she gets there? What would she use to dig the hole? How long would it take to dig a hole that deep?

38

DATE:_____ /_____ /_____

❑ *What is the best tasting thing you have ever eaten?*

WHAT TO EXPECT

This is a good question to ask on one of those days when the family seems in a nontalkative mood. Young children in your family are apt to name something they ate within the last week or two, usually something pretty conventional, like chocolate ice cream. Eight-year-olds might stretch their memory as far back as a year. They could name something they ate at a friend's house that they had never eaten before. Older kids might just make something up as a spoof and describe it in great detail; it might even be something everyone knows would be terrible, like angleworm pie (there is nothing as good as grabbing everyone's attention!).

Keep the Conversation Going by . . .

Showing your interest in what your child is saying. Let him know what you think about his delicious food choice. Where did he eat that? When was the last time he ate that? What exactly made that food item so amazing? Would he eat it every single day if he could? Why? Tell your child about the best tasting thing you've ever eaten and see if he'd like to try it too.

DATE:_____ /_____ /_____

❑ *If you could have any job in the world*
   when you grow up, what would you like
   to be?

WHAT TO EXPECT

It is never too early for your children to start thinking
about long-term goals and what they want to be when
they grow up. It will be interesting for you to hear
what your children are thinking about. It will also be
beneficial for younger children in the family, who have
limited knowledge about jobs, to listen to their older
siblings' choices. You will be surprised to discover that
even your youngest child has given this question some
thought, but should expect a restricted range of possibilities due to lack of exposure. Don't be surprised
if your son wants to be a cowboy or your daughter
wants to be a soccer player. Also, your children will get
the most out of the conversation if you do not select
your current job, but share other jobs that you seriously considered.

Keep the Conversation Going by . . .

Asking your child why she would like to have that job.
Will it be fun? What perks would the job have? What
does it take to get that kind of job? What about the job
will be difficult? Whatever your child says, just remember to be supportive. After all, there are no wrong
answers at the dinner table.

DATE:_____ /_____ /_____

❏ *What are all of the uses you can think of for bubble gum?*

WHAT TO EXPECT

At first, you should expect everyone in your family to draw a blank. After all, bubble gum is to be chewed. What else could one do with it? But slowly, ideas will start to flow. The first ideas will be straightforward, like using it to post notes on the refrigerator door. Then the more creative ideas will flow and with a bit of luck, the trickle will become a torrent. Sometimes it is fun to let one's imagination roam free. This question should get everyone throwing out zany but creative ideas. Sharing ideas and laughing together will help the family bond together closely.

Keep the Conversation Going by . . .

Encouraging your child to think outside the box. What can she do with grape bubble gum that she couldn't do with regular bubble gum? What would be the best kind of bubble gum for her project? Does she think your family could make some money by going in the bubble gum business and marketing it for that use? Be sure to inject some of your own crazy ideas into the mix.

DATE: _____ / _____ / _____

❏ *If you could have an extra body part—another leg, eye, arm, etc.—what extra body part would you want and where would you want it?*

WHAT TO EXPECT

We tend not to think much about redesigning the human body, but it can make for some interesting speculation. Your children might come up with some fascinating redesigns. Expect everyone in the family to be able to readily contribute to this conversation. Since almost any named extra body part would have some advantage, one person's answer will be as good as the next person's answer, even if there is an age difference. Younger kids will be more likely to focus on things that will immediately and directly benefit them, such as using an extra hand to allow them to brush their teeth while they do their homework or cut their meat while they eat their potatoes.

Keep the Conversation Going by . . .

Asking your child how the extra body part would be beneficial. What could he do with that extra body part? Where would he like the extra body part to be placed? For example, what about having an eye in the back of the head so he could see things coming up behind him? Would there be any disadvantages to having that extra body part? Maybe the eye would get in the way of a beloved baseball hat or make brushing your hair difficult?

DATE:_____ /_____ /_____

❏ *How many different uses can you find for a cardboard box?*

WHAT TO EXPECT

It is difficult to think outside of the box, figuratively and, in this case, literally. But learning to be a flexible thinker is a useful mental skill. The ability to think outside of the box is loosely correlated with age. The adults at your table can do it better than the children, and the older children can do it more easily than the younger children. However, as various members of the family catch on, the conversation should pick up. It is all but certain that, after the discussion has gone on for a while, family members will start to get more creative and come up with uses for the box that no one would have imagined only five minutes ago. Younger children might start with simple ideas, such as using it to store doll clothes, and then come up with bigger ideas once they hear what others are suggesting.

Keep the Conversation Going by . . .

Asking your child to push her thinking further. Yes, she could use a cardboard box for X, Y, and Z, but what would happen if it got wet? What would happen if it caught on fire? How would she work to solve those potential problems? Continue to push the envelope by asking your child what she could do with the box if she cut it up. Ask how a box could be used on the moon, in a ping pong ball factory, or at a recycling center.

DATE: _____ / _____ / _____

❑ *What is one thrilling thing that you have never done but would like to do?*

WHAT TO EXPECT

This question will prompt your kids to think about all of the exciting activities and adventures that the big, wide world has to offer. For example, would your child find it thrilling to scuba dive or has she ever wanted to fly an airplane? Almost without exception, your child has thought about something thrilling and adventure-some he or she would like to do. Some of those ideas will sound like short-term flights of fantasy. However, you may well hear an idea that a child has considered for quite some time. Asking this question might even launch a dream that will give focus and direction to a young life and you may be able to identify a strong, sincere interest of your own.

Keep the Conversation Going by . . .

Asking your child why he is interested in trying that activity. Will it be fun? Will it be scary? Will it be exhila-rating? Does he know anyone who has tried that? Does he think he'll actually be able to do that some day? If he has the opportunity to try it out, who would he like to go with him? A friend? A sibling? Why would he choose that particular person? Share your own ideas of what you'd like to try with your children during this conversation.

DATE:_____/_____/_____

❑ *If our family entered a contest to invent a new ice cream flavor, what ice cream flavor would we invent?*

WHAT TO EXPECT

Ben and Jerry's, the world famous ice cream makers in Vermont, hires people to invent different flavors of ice cream. These flavor inventors are told to let their imaginations soar. So shall it be with your family. After a few minutes of silence, you should expect your children to begin to suggest some flavors. Each new suggestion will be crazier than the last one as they build off of each other's ideas in a cooperative way. For example, your son might say, "Let's invent some ice cream that tastes like hamburgers." Your daughter may add, "Yeah, hamburgers with cheese." You might say, "What about adding BBQ sauce?"

Keep the Conversation Going by . . .

Asking your child whom he thinks would eat his ice cream. Would it be popular? What toppings would people want to add to that particular type of ice cream? For example, if your child chose hamburger ice cream, would pickles or onions be an appropriate topping? What does your child want to name his new ice cream flavor? How would he get people to buy his product? Feel free to get creative! You could vote on which of your newly created flavors would be most popular in your family.

DATE:_____ /_____ /_____

❑ *Out of everything you own, what one possession is the most important to you?*

WHAT TO EXPECT

By asking this question, you open the door for everyone in your family to learn what is most important for everyone else, which should increase their respect for these possessions. Your children will also gain insight into each person's value system. There is apt to be a wide diversity within the family of the kinds of things each person values and the reasons they value it, so you should expect that no answer will be the same. Younger children will most likely choose a favorite toy, such as a stuffed bear. Kids between six and ten may have an object that is important, such as a signed hockey puck, coin collection, or special souvenir from a trip, show, or outing.

Keep the Conversation Going by . . .

Encouraging your child to tell you why this particular possession is so important to her. When did she get it? How did she happen to get it? If she lost it, is there anything that could replace it? Ask other members of the family to let your child know how they feel about her item—or if they even knew it was that important to her. Be sure to talk about your most treasured item during this conversation.

DATE:_____ /_____ /_____

❑ *Out of the people you know, do you know anyone who recently had their feelings hurt or who had a particularly rough week?*

WHAT TO EXPECT

Your young children don't attend to others' feelings, so it will be good for them to hear you talk about and express empathy for people they know who have had a rough week. Once a model has been set, all of the children at the dinner table will be able, at least on some level, to look outside of themselves to recall something bad that happened to someone else and possibly even to express empathy. Children under six might recall a big brother stubbing his toe. Children between six and eleven will be able to talk about a friend getting grounded or a parent who lost something important. By asking this conversation starter, you will start the process of teaching your children to see the world from other people's perspectives.

Keep the Conversation Going by . . .

Asking your child how he knew that person had something bad happen to him or her or had his or her feelings hurt. What did he see or hear that told him that? Did the person seem sad? Angry? Frazzled? Was he able to help that person?

DATE:_____ /_____ /_____

❑ *What do you worry about the most?*

WHAT TO EXPECT

One on hand, this conversation starter might alert you to concerns and worries that are profoundly troubling your children, such as fear of death or of the dark. On the other, the benign concerns and worries mentioned may assure you that all is okay, such as worries about forgetting homework. If your children have no serious worries, this will be a light-hearted conversation. However, if someone voices a serious worry, don't minimize his or her concern by saying, "It will get better soon, especially if you stop worrying about it." Instead, just listen and validate your child's feelings.

Keep the Conversation Going by . . .

Remembering that self-disclosure is a great way to break the ice. Share something that is worrying you now or that worried you when you were the child's age. How did you deal with your worry? How did it affect your life? Let your child know that everything turned out okay in the end.

DATE:_____ /_____ /_____

☐ *What one thing would you change about the world we live in?*

WHAT TO EXPECT

By listening to adults answer this question, your younger children will be introduced to the idea of societal responsibility. There will probably be a wide range in the seriousness and gravity of the conversation. Your children may have differences picking the one thing that is most critical, which can be a good thing. It gives the adults an opportunity to model respect for other people's opinions. If the question proves to be beyond a child's developmental level, accept with a smile whatever he says, even if what he says is that, "Everyone in the world should have a skateboard."

Keep the Conversation Going by . . .

Questioning your kids a bit more about their chosen change. Who would benefit from the change? Would it only be your child, your family, or everyone in the world? Why is that particular change important to your child? Answer these questions about the change that you chose also.

DATE: _____ / _____ / _____

❏ *What helps you feel better when something bad happens to you?*

WHAT TO EXPECT

Learning that one can do specific things to make themselves feel better is an understanding that develops slowly throughout childhood. For example, when something bad happens to a four-year-old, it's likely that she will cry and the parent will come to give solace. By age six, when something bad happens, most children will seek out a parent and cry in their presence. However, by age ten, children start to think that they should tough it out when something bad happens to them. After all, they don't see their parents cry. This developmental sequence makes this a particularly good question and you should expect your children to offer answers that tie into it. It will encourage each child to get in touch with what he or she can do to feel better when something bad happens.

Keep the Conversation Going by . . .

Asking your child to reflect back on the last bad day she had. Was she able to do something that made her day improve on her own or did someone else help her feel better? Tell your child about one of the worst days you've ever had and what you did to make yourself feel better. In giving your answer, you may want to slant your solution to suggest something that is age appropriate for your child, and then ask if she thinks that technique would work for her.

DATE: _____ / _____ / _____

❑ *How do you show your friends that you care about them?*

WHAT TO EXPECT

This question will likely cause even the adults at the table to realize that they do not intentionally do enough to demonstrate their regard for others, and it will also prompt them to consider what they might do in the future. Expect each of your children to share stories of times they spent caring for friends, which may carry over to a discussion of caring within the family. If you have children eight and younger, they are apt to say that they show their friends they care about them by sharing toys. Children around the age of ten will say that they show their friends they care about them by doing things together. Teenagers are likely to say that they show their friends that they care about them by listening to them.

Keep the Conversation Going by . . .

Making sure your child knows how proud you are of him for caring for his friends. Then ask him about the last time he did something to show a friend that he cared about him or her. What exactly did he do? How did that friend respond to his gesture? How did he feel when he did something to show his friend how much he cares? Did the friend do something nice back? How did your child feel when his friend was nice to him?

DATE:_____ /_____ /_____

❏ *If you could paint your room any color, what color would you choose?*

WHAT TO EXPECT

Expect your younger children to blurt out a color immediately and girls often go with pink or purple whereas boys are more likely to choose gray or black. Older children will give the question more thought and as the family discusses the possibilities, you might hear some creative answers involving stripes or patterns, as well as paint on the ceiling.

Keep the Conversation Going by . . .

Asking why your child chose that color. How does that color make her feel? Does she think she would like to live with that color for years or would she like to change the color often? Talk about the colors you like in rooms in your home and what colors you would like to change or add.

DATE:_____ /_____ /_____

❑ *Our family is hosting a radio talk show! What topic would you like us to discuss on the air?*

WHAT TO EXPECT

Children under the age of nine might suggest that the talk show be about pets, favorite books, or the latest video games. They will like the idea of hosting the show and steering the direction of it. They will be most excited about topics of interest to them personally. You can expect children ten to thirteen to be more practical. They might suggest a talk show about how to train dogs or how to fix cars. Adolescents might suggest a talk show about exciting people or places and will be more interested in interviews.

Keep the Conversation Going by . . .

Having your child tell you more about his show's details. Who would listen to his talk show? What role would each family member play on the show? What would everyone's radio name be? What would your family do to keep the listening audience glued to the radio? Would your child invite the audience to write in with questions or comments? If he did, what might they write? Practice using a radio voice.

DATE:_____ / _____ / _____

❑ ***On a scale of one to ten, with one being terrible and ten being outstanding, what kind of day did you have?***

WHAT TO EXPECT

Your family members will likely take some time to reflect on their days. In doing so, they will also think about the specific things that impacted the day. Everyone should be able to readily contribute to this conversation. The younger children will tend to hop on whatever band-wagon comes down the road. If an older sibling tells about having a terrible day, the younger child will have had a worse day. If the older sibling tells of having a great day, the younger child will have had a better day. Young children will have a hard time with the one to ten scale and will probably overestimate how good or bad the day really was.

Keep the Conversation Going by . . .

Encouraging your child to tell you what made it that kind of day. Was there anything she did that made it that kind of day, or did it just happen? Using the same scale of one to ten, have your child tell you what kind of a day she had yesterday and what kind of a day she thinks she'll have tomorrow. Make sure you talk to your family about the type of day you had as well.

DATE:_____ /_____ /_____

❑ *Tell us about a time when someone lied to you.*

WHAT TO EXPECT

Sometimes things that adults regard as small issues trouble children a lot. If your child is deeply upset because he feels someone has lied to him, this conversation will give that issue a chance to surface. This is a dicey topic. It is possible that someone will tell about an upsetting, serious lie—and the liar might be at the table. If that is the case, don't allow the accused liar to defend himself. Instead, just say, "This is not your story to tell. Let's just listen to your brother's or sister's story."

Keep the Conversation Going by . . .

Asking your child to tell the family more about how that lie made him feel. Does he think that the person who lied to him knew she was telling a lie? Has he ever lied to the person who lied to him? How does he think that made that person feel? Ask your child to tell you exactly what he thinks a lie is and explain the difference—and the similarity—between a whopper and a little white lie. You can share stories about lies that have been told to you as well.

DATE:_____ / _____ / _____

❑ *How do your friends help you be a better person?*

WHAT TO EXPECT

Adults and older children are likely to reflect on their past friends. Their discussion will help your children learn the importance of networking, and help them see that even now they are forming friendships that will last a lifetime. Expect everyone at the table to be able to contribute to this conversation, but realize that adults will have the most to say, mentioning people and recalling events that no one else in the family had previously known anything about. Once that model of reflection has been set, older children will find some specific things that their friends do to help them. For example one may say, "Erica helps me study for the spelling test and sometimes she shows me how to remember the way a word is spelled." Younger children will have to dig deep to come up with something, but they will. For example, "Sally sometimes tells me when I am not following the rules."

Keep the Conversation Going by . . .

Having your child tell you what being a good person means to her and then asking if she thinks her friends are good people. Why does she think this? What does she like best about her particular group of friends? How does your child think she helps her friends be better people as well? Ask why friends should help each other.

DATE:_____ /_____ /_____

❏ *What is your biggest fear?*

WHAT TO EXPECT

Expect to glean a lot of valuable information from this simple conversation starter. Your children's answers will tell you whether the thing they are afraid of is in the past or in the present. More importantly, you'll be able to tell whether your child's fears stem from an active, creative imagination (such as monsters under the bed) or something more serious (fear of swimming) that you'll need to address. If your child's fears are normal and thus benign, this will be a light-hearted conversation. Just by talking about the fear, the child will recognize it is not a serious threat. However, avoid minimizing your child's fears. If you make light of something your child is really afraid of, she may feel that you are discounting her feelings.

Keep the Conversation Going by . . .

Letting your child know that everyone is afraid of something and that it's okay for him to talk about his fears. Ask him if he has encountered this fear or if it is just something that might happen. What was the scariest moment of his life? Be sure to let him know what you are afraid of and let him know the moment when you were the most afraid.

DATE:_____ / _____ / _____

❑ *If you could travel anywhere in the world
for a week-long visit, where would you go?*

WHAT TO EXPECT

This conversation might reveal knowledge and interests that no one was aware of and you should expect
to get a sense of your children's understanding of the
world. Children will probably want to go somewhere
that they can have fun and that they are familiar with
through TV, such as Disney World. However, young
people today are amazingly aware of the world. Don't
be surprised if they want to go someplace they heard
about in the news, in movies, or through multimedia.

Keep the Conversation Going by . . .

Asking your child where she learned about the place
she wants to visit. Why would she want to go there?
What does she want to learn and see and explore
there? Ask her how much she knows about that place
already. Where else is she interested in going?

DATE:_____ /_____ /_____

❑ *Imagine yourself ten years from now.*
What will you be doing?

WHAT TO EXPECT

This conversation starter will force your children to think about upcoming changes. The realization that in ten years their lives will have changed significantly will be sure to surprise them. Usually, only those members of the family sitting on the cusp of change, such as parents getting ready to change jobs, children getting ready to go to new schools, or families getting ready to relocate, will have thought much about what the next ten years will bring. So after doing the math and giving it some thought, a seven-year-old child may say, "Gosh. I guess I'll be in high school. I'll really like being able to drive a car."

Keep the Conversation Going by . . .

Talking to your child about his expectations for his future. What is he most excited about in the future? Does he need to start doing anything today to get to that point? What are some of the goals that he has set for himself? If you have a younger child, go along with what he says (after all there are no right or wrong answers) and let him know that his future can be whatever he wants it to be.

DATE: _____ / _____ / _____

❑ *What are three things that you love?*

WHAT TO EXPECT

Your children will think about the things that are important to them and what gives them pleasure and happiness. When talking about things they love, expect younger children to mention activities or tangible items, such as toys. Children over age nine are likely to mention friends, activities they do with their peers, and music. Adults tend to take a more reflective approach. They will often talk about loving a particular person, loving some facet of their work, or loving hobbies such as hunting, fishing, or visiting with friends.

Keep the Conversation Going by . . .

Having your child tell you why she loves those things. Does she think other people in the family love those things too? What else does she love? Have her list as many things as she can possibly think of in two minutes. Talk about what she comes up with.

TAKE A TIP:
KEEP THE DISCUSSION LIVELY

It isn't necessary to comment after each child contributes to the discussion, but you may occasionally need to interject a comment or two to maintain the flow of conversation. Use these five tips to keep the discussion lively:

1. Paraphrase. Paraphrasing lets the person know you understood them. Hearing a restatement of what someone has said gives others time to formulate their thoughts

2. Compliment a thoughtful or insightful comment. You should never miss an opportunity to affirm a child's good efforts and contributions to the conversation. It doesn't take much and just saying "Good idea" is enough reinforcement.

3. Summarize the major ideas that have been generated. This will help you keep the conversation focused. You can also identify the important points for the younger members of the family.

4. Mediate and encourage different opinions. In this context, mediation means that when two family members have a different perspective or opinion, you find something of value in each position and share it.

5. Draw out those who haven't spoken yet. This has to be done carefully. Saying, "Josh, it's your turn to talk," won't do it. Instead, try saying something like, "Josh, I'd really to hear what you think about that."

DATE:_____ /_____ /_____

❑ *If you could be any type of dinosaur, what kind would you like to be?*

WHAT TO EXPECT

Younger children may be familiar with only a few types and are likely to latch on to the ones that have been the most memorable for them, such as T-Rex and brontosaurus. Older children probably have a broader knowledge and may choose lesser known dinosaurs.

Keep the Conversation Going by . . .

Asking your child why he chose that particular dinosaur. Ask him to describe the kinds of things that dinosaur did that he would like to do. Encourage him to do an impersonation of his favorite dinosaurs. You could talk about the different theories about why dinosaurs are now extinct to continue the conversation.

DATE:_____ /_____ /_____

❑ *If you could build your own house, what would it be like?*

WHAT TO EXPECT

This question allows children to use their imaginations. Younger kids will probably have wild ideas about things such as trampoline rooms, kitchens with built-in slushie machines, and indoor pools. Those of your children over ten will be more thoughtful and interested in more realistic possibilities, such as hot tubs and game rooms. As everyone bounces their ideas around, you'll probably pick up on what kinds of activities are important to each child.

Keep the Conversation Going By . . .

Asking your child for details about why she chose each amenity. What would her bedroom be like? How many rooms would the house have? Would there be anything special for the family pet? What's the most important thing the house should have? Share your ideas about what you would love to have in your own dream home.

62

DATE:_____/_____/_____

❑ *Name one person who has made a differ-ence in your life.*

WHAT TO EXPECT

When discussing this question, it is a good idea for you to go first and offer an example of how someone has made a difference in your life. Tell your kids how this person changed you or something in your life so that it made a difference. Suggest that there are lots of ways people can make a difference. Older children will likely come up with some answers first and might share thoughts about a minister, coach, or teacher who has encouraged them or helped them through a hard time. Younger children will have a harder time with this question, but it is still an important exercise for them. Expect them to talk about a memorable moment that an adult was involved in, such as the coach when she won the soccer game or the principal when she par-ticipated in the spelling bee.

Keep the Conversation Going by . . .

Having your child tell you what that person did that made a difference in her life. This question may cause her to think about whether she ever let that person know how much he or she made a difference. Ask her if she thinks that she might want to make a difference in someone else's life. What could she do to make a difference?

DATE:_____ /_____ /_____

❑ *What do you think would be the best thing about being the oldest person in the family?*

WHAT TO EXPECT

This conversation starter will force your children to try on the shoes of the oldest person in the family (likely you or your partner, but it could be extended to grandparents and so on) and attempt to look at the advantages—and the responsibilities—that are incumbent on the person who fills this role. Younger children are apt to see only the advantages of being the oldest in the family. After all, no one tells the oldest person in the family what to do. Older children are more likely to see some of the responsibilities that accompany being the oldest person in the family.

Keep the Conversation Going by . . .

Asking your child what the oldest person in the family may like about being the oldest. Then ask what the best thing would be about being the youngest person in the family. If the youngest is sitting at the table, have him tell you what he likes and dislikes about it. Would it be good to be neither the youngest nor the oldest? Talk about your feelings as a child about your place in your family.

DATE:_____ /_____ /_____

❑ *If you were going to move out of this
house right now and live somewhere else,
where would you go?*

WHAT TO EXPECT

The thought of this might be a little overwhelming to
your children at first, but you can expect children under
six to have some unrealistic and fun ideas. They might
want to go to the moon, the bottom of the ocean, or
to Disney World. Don't be surprised if your child says
there is nowhere else she would want to live, since the
thought of this can be overwhelming for some. Children
over ten will have more realistic ideas, such as Florida,
Hawaii, or another country.

Keep the Conversation Going by . . .

Having your child give you details about the new place
she will live. Why would she choose to live there? Will
this place be near the beach? What would she like
about it? What would she dislike? Ask her what she
will miss about the place where you are currently living.

DATE:_____ /_____ /_____

❑ *You have been hired to create a television commercial to sell a new car. What would you say about the car to get people to buy it?*

WHAT TO EXPECT

Children under six will talk about how fast the car goes, how cool it looks, and what color it is. They're focused on the most immediate and exciting features and are likely to think of cars in the same way they think of toys. They want to talk about the things that immediately appeal to them. Children over ten have more knowledge about cars and will likely talk about gas mileage, price, and features like heated seats.

Keep the Conversation Going by . . .

Asking your child why he thinks people buy certain cars. Does the color of the car matter? What kind of car would he like to have? What types of things does he like on the inside of a car? What kind of commercial would make him want to buy it? You can talk about why you bought your current car or what you would look for in a car.

DATE: _____ / _____ / _____

☐ *What do you think it would be like to be a member of a minority race in our community? (Or, what is it like being a minority in our community?)*

WHAT TO EXPECT

If your family is not a minority, your children under eight may really have no idea that minorities face discrimination and you will need to explain how minorities are sometimes treated unfairly. You can make it real by asking your child what it would be like if everyone in your child's school wearing a red shirt was treated unfairly. Your children will focus on how unfair and wrong that would be and probably become outraged. Children over eight will have some understanding of minority issues and will be able to point out how some people treat minorities poorly.

Keep the Conversation Going by . . .

Asking if your child has a friend or knows anyone who is a member of a minority community. In what ways is that person similar to him? Do they like to hang out together? Play games? Have sleepovers? Are there any differences other than appearances that your child can think of? What are the advantages to being different?

DATE:_____ /_____ /_____

❏ *What is the one thing you've done that got you in the most trouble?*

WHAT TO EXPECT

Children will talk about things they did at home or at school that got them in the most trouble and are the most memorable to them based on the reaction or punishment they got. They may feel shy about bringing the incident up again and worried you will again chastise them, so be sure to say that you're just interested in hearing how they feel about it and are not going to get mad or upset. By sharing your own stories with them, your children will start to see you as real people who were young once and once did the same or similar foolish things that they sometimes do. They are likely to be relieved to know that and this knowledge may cause them to open up.

Keep the Conversation Going by . . .

Asking your child to tell you why he decided to do the thing that got him in trouble. Was he curious? Did he know that it was wrong? If so, why did he decide to do it anyway? How did he feel about the punishment or consequences? Would he do it again?

DATE: _____ / _____ / _____

❑ *What would you like to have written on your headstone when you pass on?*

WHAT TO EXPECT

This question could be hard for children under six who don't have a good understanding or acceptance of death. If it seems the question is upsetting, change the topic to something else. Frame the question by telling them some interesting, weird, funny, or nice things you've seen on headstones, such as "I told you I was sick" or "Pardon me for not rising." Children will enjoy the humor aspect and will try to come up with their own. Older children and teens will take the question more seriously and think about more serious epitaphs.

Keep the Conversation Going by . . .

Asking your child why she would choose that epitaph. What does it say about her? If she forgets to write her own epitaph, what might someone else write about her to sum up her life? Why do people put epitaphs on gravestones? Does it help people in remembering the person who is gone? If so, how?

DATE:_____ /_____ /_____

❑ *If you could give one person a special gift, to whom would you give that gift and what would you give?*

WHAT TO EXPECT

Children will probably initially think about gifts for friends or close family members and will focus on things they would like to receive, such as toys or food. You and your older children can help redirect the conversation to thinking about special gifts that have meaning. Talk about a special gift that had meaning to you as an example. Then suggest your child try to think of a special gift he could give to Grandma, an elderly neighbor, or a teacher.

Keep the Conversation Going by . . .

Asking your a child why she chose that particular person and that particular gift. What did that person do to deserve the gift? Why would your child give that particular gift? Does the gift represent something to either her or the person she wants to give it to?

DATE: _____ / _____ / _____

❑ *If you could live anywhere—truly any-where; it could be on Earth, in outer space, or in a fictional world—where would you live?*

WHAT TO EXPECT

This is an opportunity for free association and cre-ativity, so expect your children to jump right in. Young children are apt to select the last place that they saw recently on television and can pronounce, such as the North Pole. As the discussion gets going, your kids will think more creatively and you'll hear ideas about living on Mars, living in a cartoon world, or life in a universe where everything is polka-dotted and people only eat hamburgers. Children over ten will have more certain ideas about where they would go and may draw on books or movies they've recently seen.

Keep the Conversation Going by . . .

Having your child tell you why she would like to live there. How did she learn about or imagine that place? If it's a real place, does she think she might actually go there some day? What would the benefits be of living in the place your child chose? For example, if she chose outer space, maybe weightlessness could be an advantage. What are the disadvantages? Maybe the cold would be a disadvantage of living at the North Pole? Make sure your child's imagination leads the way through this conversation starter.

DATE: _____ / _____ / _____

❑ *A lot of people have weird physical abilities. Some can wiggle their ears, cross their eyes, or roll their tongues. What is your weirdest physical talent?*

WHAT TO EXPECT

Your children will probably start out by saying "I can go like this" and make a face, twist their arm, or stick out their tongue in a funny way. As the conversation continues and you and older children talk, younger children might focus on something they realize they can do and no one else at the table can do. This discussion will help them focus in on individual characteristics their bodies may have and help them become more self-aware.

Keep the Conversation Going by . . .

Asking what weird physical talent your child wishes she had. Why? Does she think these are things that can be learned or are they things people are born being able to do? What does it say about how different we all are?

DATE:_____ /_____ /_____

❑ *What is one thing about yourself you
think everyone in the family should know?*

WHAT TO EXPECT

This conversation starter presents the opportunity
for family members to tell something about themselves that they see as important and want recognized.
Expect children nine and younger to share something
that everyone already knows, such as "I love dogs" or
"I like to draw pictures." Children in the ten year and
older range might give this a lot of thought and share
something that family members really don't know, such
as "I want to be a biologist." As you talk about things
about yourself that might not be so obvious, younger
kids will follow your drift and be a bit more revealing
themselves. This helps everyone in the family come to
understand each other on a deeper level and encourages introspection.

Keep the Conversation Going by . . .

Encouraging your child to tell you a little more about
why he thinks that is an important piece of information about him. Does he think there are things like this
about all people? Does knowing this piece of information help everyone in the family understand him better
in his opinion? What other things should your family
know about him?

DATE:_____ /_____ /_____

❑ *What have you learned from someone who is from a different culture or race?*

WHAT TO EXPECT

Anything that is different often can be scary; but to encourage appreciation of differences, ask children to focus on the wonderful things they've learned from a friend who comes from a different background. Children are apt to talk about someone they know in their class who is of a different race or religion. Older family members are likely to have had more exposure to people of different backgrounds and can help children learn by giving examples of things that they've learned about different cultures and customs. For example, maybe someone in your family has a Native American friend and can tell your child that people from the Navajo culture face their doors to the east, toward the rising sun. Children are usually very interested in learning about these differences and find them fascinating, but may ask "Why?"

Keep the Conversation Going by . . .

Asking your child to tell you more about what she has learned from her friend. Does her friend eat any foods that your child was unfamiliar with? Did she have to do anything differently when she went to play at her friend's house? Maybe she had to take her shoes off or observe a moment of silence before dinner? Did learning that help her understand her friend any better? Does she think her friend has learned anything different from her?

DATE:_____ /_____ /_____

□ *When you are the happiest, what are you doing and who are you with?*

WHAT TO EXPECT

Young children will initially offer everyday scenarios, such as "When I'm playing Barbies" or "When I'm riding my bike." It takes some discussion for them to think more widely about the question and identify who they are with when they are happiest. They will often then identify a friend or parent who does fun or exciting things with them and may point to specific examples, such as "When Daddy took me ice skating." Discussion by you and your older children will be deeper and focus more on the people than the activities.

Keep the Conversation Going By . . .

Asking your child why this makes him happy. Have him tell you about a time when he tried to arrange things to make himself happy. Did it work? If not, why? Could he have done things differently? When does he think other family members are at their happiest?

DATE:_____ /_____ /_____

❑ *What are some of the qualities that make you a good friend?*

WHAT TO EXPECT

Each family member will need to be introspective about themselves and how they relate with others. The older folks at the table, who know what it means to be a good friend, may have to examine themselves before answering this question, but most children will not hesitate. Expect them to say that they let other kids play with their toys; they play with friends on the swings; and if they have some candy, they share it.

Keep the Conversation Going by . . .

Encouraging your child to talk about all of his good qualities. Does he share? Help other kids when they need him? Let his younger sibling have the last cookie? Ask him what his friends would say about him if they were there. Does he make an effort to be a good friend, or does it just come naturally? Be sure to point out to your child things that you see him do that make him a good friend.

DATE:_____ /_____ /_____

❑ *What is your favorite piece of clothing or outfit?*

WHAT TO EXPECT

Your children will have definite opinions about this and will pick a piece of clothing that they see as important at the moment and that reflects their interests. If your daughter is completely into horses, her horse t-shirt may be her pick. If your son is a sports fan, his hockey jersey may be his pick. The item your child chooses will show you how he identifies or sees himself at this point in his life. Older kids will choose items that cement their social status or identity, such as a shirt with the hottest label.

Keep the Conversation Going by . . .

Asking your child why that is her favorite item or out-fit. How does she feel when she wears it? If she could buy any piece of clothing to be her new favorite item, what would it be? Why? Start a discussion about why clothes are so important to us. What do they tell you about someone? Be sure to talk about your own favor-ite piece of clothing and the reasons behind it.

DATE:_____ /_____ /_____

❑ *What if our family was going on vacation and you were in charge of bringing all the fun things to do. What would you pack?*

WHAT TO EXPECT

It is important to empower children. Even a pretend assignment is empowering. You can expect that the children's ability to think about the needs and interests of others will develop with age. The answers will tell you quite a bit about what your children value, their aptitude to plan, their ability to understand the need to plan for the unexpected, and their capacity to think about others. You can expect young children to first want to pack the things they see as the most fun— games, toys, electronics, etc. As you talk more, they might expand their ideas about what "fun" items are and think to pack the family pet, the TV, their bikes, and more.

Keep the Conversation Going by . . .

Asking your child what his dream vacation would be. Would he be happier on the beach or in the snow? What if you were going to Mount Everest? Would that change his list of things to bring? What if you were going to a deserted island with no electricity? How would he have fun without TV, radios, or video games? Is there a particular person with whom he would like to go on vacation?

DATE:_____ /_____ /_____

❑ ***Would you rather live on the moon, in the ocean, or on a cloud?***

WHAT TO EXPECT

NASA scientists have given serious consideration to colonizing the moon, and one of the star attractions of the 1964 New York World's Fair was an exhibit showing people living underwater. However, living on a cloud is mostly considered wishful thinking, as in "he's living on Cloud Nine." That's why it's fun for kids to discuss these options. Your child will pick the thing that appeals to him most off the bat without thinking it through carefully. Older children might see the real possibilities, taking the conversation to a higher level.

Keep the Conversation Going by . . .

Having your child tell you more about her plans. Would she be the only one living wherever she decides or would there be entire cities? Would she have a house to live in? What would it look like? What would be the best thing about her chosen option? Why did she choose that place to live over the others? How would she stay in touch with you if you stayed right here on firm land?

DATE:_____ /_____ /_____

❑ *If you could go on a sleepover anywhere in the country, where would you go and what would you do?*

WHAT TO EXPECT

Children go on sleepovers to their aunt's, their grand-mother's, or most often at a friend's house. But a sleepover in a museum, an amusement park, a movie theater, the subway in New York City, or Yellowstone National Park would be much different. This question appeals to children's imaginations, so expect them to be exited about answering and to wonder what the experience would be like. Young children won't be interested in considering comfort, so don't be surprised if your child suggests a sleepover on top of the Empire State Building or in an aquarium.

Keep the Conversation Going by . . .

Encouraging your child to tell why he would like to have a sleepover there. What is it that makes that place seem fun, exciting, and different? Since no one sleeps at a sleepover, what would your child do? Why does doing things at night when it's dark seem more exciting than doing them during the day? Who would your child want to go with him on this sleepover? What would he pack?

DATE:_____ /_____ /_____

❑ *Who in our family would do the best job being President of the United States?*

WHAT TO EXPECT

This question requires children to consider and affirm the qualities of other family members. Many young children secretly wonder, especially at election time, whether they might grow up to become the President of the United States, so don't be surprised if your child nominates himself! Expect a light-hearted conversation with laughter and maybe even some good-natured joking, like "Dad's graying hair might convince the voters he has wisdom." Older family members will probably give serious consideration to the qualities or characteristics of a good president. However, guard against the conversation focusing on just one person.

Keep the Conversation Going by . . .

Asking your child to back up her selection with specifics. For example, if your child says, "Uncle Jim would be the best President because he's brave," you may want to ask her what it is about Uncle Jim that makes him seem brave. Also, ask your child how your family would get the public to vote for her choice. Does she think her choice would actually get elected? Would she like to be the President herself?

DATE:_____ / _____ / _____

❑ *What is your favorite joke? Tell it to us.*

WHAT TO EXPECT

Telling a joke well takes practice, but it is a good social skill. This is a good time for children to learn the art of telling a joke and coming to understand a joke's social value. Expect some of the jokes to be funny, but understand that some won't be. The very youngest child could repeat an off-color joke that he or she overheard but did not understand. If that happens, label it as a joke that might offend some people and ask the next person to tell his or her joke. Knock-knock jokes are some of the simplest and easiest to remember, so expect to hear some from your young children, and don't be surprised if your child messes up the punch line.

Keep the Conversation Going by . . .

Asking your child where he heard that joke. What makes a joke funny to him? What does he find funny about that particular joke? Be sure to reciprocate when asking this question; your child will want to hear your jokes as well.

DATE: _____ / _____ / _____

❑ *If you could get your face painted right now, what would your face painting look like?*

WHAT TO EXPECT
Expect your kids to crank up their imaginations and describe some interesting things they would have painted on their faces. Younger children are likely to think about painting their face with a common symbol such as a sun, moon, star, bolt of lightning, or heart. Older children might go for a face painting that has mild shock value, like tattoos they have seen.

Keep the Conversation Going by . . .
Asking your child if she would like her whole face or just a part of her face painted. If she wanted her whole face painted, would she want a scary face or a happy face? What colors would she like to include in her face painting? Why those colors? Where would she go to show off your face painting? What would people think of it?

DATE:_____ / _____ / _____

❑ *What does your bedroom say about who you are?*

WHAT TO EXPECT

Parents often decorate the bedrooms of their infants and preschool children, and the decorations usually make a statement. But, as children get older, they add their own touches. Young children might say that the room shows they like a certain color or like things the room is decorated with, such as trucks or cowboys. You might also expect them to say something simple like "I'm a girl" or "I'm six." Older children will relate personality traits that the room demonstrates.

Keep the Conversation Going by . . .

Asking your child to tell you what items in her bedroom tell the most about who she is as a person. Does her pink lamp tell of her love of ballet? Do the soccer trophies tell of her athletic achievements? Does her room say the right thing about her? An older child may feel that her bedroom is too young. If she could add something to her bedroom, what would it be?

DATE: _____ / _____ / _____

❑ *Look at the person on your right and tell that person one thing you really like about him or her.*

WHAT TO EXPECT

Acknowledging a family member's good actions encourages everyone to display more good actions, which in turn makes everyone happier. Each family member will hear something nice about him or herself, but they will also say something nice about someone else. Comments from young children might not be very sophisticated, such as "I like your hair" or "I like when you play checkers with me." Dad may say to his six-year-old, "Last week, we worked on your spelling words together, and I could see how frustrated you were. But I like that you don't give up, even when you really want to."

Keep the Conversation Going by . . .

Encourage your child to tell the table how hearing that compliment made him feel. Did he feel proud? Loved? Capable? How does he think the person that he complimented feels? Does he feel good about making that person feel good? Why? Who else has traits similar to the ones your family members have admired in each other? How would life be different if everyone said one positive thing to someone else every day?

DATE:_____ / _____ / _____

❑ *What would it be like to be seven feet tall?*

WHAT TO EXPECT

This conversation starter will force your children to consider what the world would be like if they stood in someone else's shoes—and in this case, big shoes. You should expect almost everyone to think of the advantages that tall people have in sports, especially basketball. It is unlikely that your kids will immediately think of the disadvantages of being seven feet tall.

Keep the Conversation Going by . . .

Asking your child if he wishes that he were seven feet tall. Would he play sports if he were? Can he think of any disadvantages to being seven feet tall? Maybe he would bang his head on doorframes or would have to slouch down in the car to avoid hitting his head. Would it be worth it? What would it be like if he was more than seven feet tall? What is the tallest he would like to be?

DATE:_____ /_____ /_____

❑ *Would you rather be a pirate, a cowboy/
cowgirl, or an astronaut?*

WHAT TO EXPECT

Your children watch movies, see television programs,
and read books about people who lead exciting lives
and they fantasize about what it would be like to be
those people. Asking this question should tap a reser-
voir of dreams and fantasies. Many little girls and boys
envision themselves flying off into space or riding a
horse into the sunset. Expect your child's answer to
showcase his personal fantasy.

Keep the Conversation Going by . . .

Telling your child which person you wanted to be when
you were growing up and which you would choose to
be now. Ask you child how long she's thought about
being that person. What would she like about being
a pirate, cowgirl, or astronaut? Would it be exciting?
Adventurous? Dangerous? Does she think that she'd
actually like to become any of the three in real life?

DATE: _____ / _____ / _____

❑ *What would you miss the most if we no longer had electricity?*

WHAT TO EXPECT

We take many modern conveniences for granted. This question should increase your children's appreciation of at least one of those things. Children nine-years-old and younger may not realize how much electricity improves their life. An adult should begin this conversation by thinking aloud, "Humm. If we didn't have electricity, we wouldn't have TV, lights, dishwashers, or computers. I wonder which of those things I'd miss the most." Then your children will start to add to the list of all the things in the house that plug in to run and will be able to isolate one they would miss the most.

Keep the Conversation Going by . . .

Having your child list the things she uses the most that are powered by electricity. Would she be willing to give any of them up? How would giving up that item most change her daily life? What could she use instead of electricity to do that thing? For example, instead of making cookies in her EasyBake Oven, you could help her make cookies on the grill.

DATE: _____ / _____ / _____

❑ *Where is your favorite place to hide out when you want to be by yourself?*

WHAT TO EXPECT

Each member of the family will need to be reflective and also somewhat self-disclosing, which often strengthens the family bond. The adults at the dinner table will struggle with this question more than the children because most adults do not hide out. However, we do make up excuses to go places to have some peace and quiet. Dad might go "work" in the garage. Mom might go "sew" in the bedroom. If this does not fit, the adults might tell about where they went to hide out when they were kids. Young children probably have favorite hiding places such as under their bed, in a tree, in a fort in the backyard, or behind the couch and will easily share these places. Older kids may have a harder time with the question and stick with answers like "My room."

Keep the Conversation Going by . . .

Asking your child to tell you what he likes to do when he is hiding out. Does he like to read? Draw? Play an instrument? Why does he sometimes like to hide out? Does he feel that he has enough privacy?

DATE: _____ / _____ / _____

☐ *If you had another sibling, what would you want that person to be like?*

WHAT TO EXPECT

Expect to gain some insight into what your young child's relationship needs may be within the current family organization. Your young children are apt to give the most revealing answers. Their relationship world is small, but it is evolving. Your only son might say things like "I want a brother who could play soccer with me." Your youngest might say, "I want a brother or sister who would have to do what I say."

Keep the Conversation Going by . . .

Asking if your child would like to have another sibling. What are the advantages and disadvantages? Before this, has your child ever given much thought to even having another sibling? Would she like the sibling to be similar to her or would she like the sibling to be someone completely different? Why?

DATE:_____ /_____ /_____

❑ *If you wrote a book, what would it be about?*

WHAT TO EXPECT

Remind younger kids that books can be fiction or non-fiction. You will probably hear responses that are similar to stories your children currently enjoy, but you may also get answers about things your child is interested in at the moment, such as spiders, dance, or the hottest toy. Your child might outline a plot for you which might not make a lot of sense or be very complete, but encourage and welcome this creativity and tell your child that it is a book you would like to read.

Keep the Conversation Going by . . .

Asking your child what kind of cover the book would have. What is the name of the main character, if the book your child wants to write is fiction? What would it be like to see a book that he wrote at his own school library? What is his favorite book? Why does he like that book? Talk about books you enjoy and if you've ever thought about writing a book.

DATE:_____ /_____ /_____

❑ *What is the most exciting thing that hap-*
pened to you last week?

WHAT TO EXPECT
Children under age seven will happily relate a fun thing
that happened to them that day or the day before. It
may take some thought and discussion for your child
to remember back five or six days ago, since young
children are more focused on the immediate. Children
over seven will have an easier time answering this and
may talk about finding a dollar on the street or some
other truly unexpected and exciting thing.

Keep the Conversation Going by . . .

Encouraging your child to tell you more. Where did
this thing happen? What were the circumstances? Did
he expect it to happen? Were other people involved
in this excitement or was it something that happened
just to him? How did this thing affect him? Have your
child try to guess the most exciting part of your week.

DATE: _____ / _____ / _____

❑ *If you could invite any character from a book, TV show, or movie to do something with you, whom would you invite and what would you do?*

WHAT TO EXPECT

Expect your children to enjoy stepping into the world of imagination and possibilities. However, it is the adults at the dinner table who will have the most difficulty imagining doing something with an imaginary character. Young kids will focus on a TV character, most likely a cartoon. Older children may turn to movies that they find exciting. If your child is very into a book series, you might hear about a character from that series.

Keep the Conversation Going by . . .

Having your child describe the way he'd like his day with his character to play out. Where would he like to go? Would he like to show the character his favorite things? Would he like to bring a friend along? Would your child like to spend a day in the character's world as well? What would he like to do there?

DATE:_____ /_____ /_____

❑ *If you were a super hero, what would your super power be?*

WHAT TO EXPECT

This conversation starter fits right into things that most young children have fantasized about. You can expect children eight and younger to really get into this conversation. They will love to talk about having a super power. As children get older, they get more mature and may say it's stupid to think about having a super power because there is no such thing. If your children respond this way, ask them to take a power they already have (like eyesight) and think about it being particularly powerful (like eyes that could see a fly a block away).

Keep the Conversation Going by . . .

Having your child tell you more about what she would do with that super power. Would she use it only for good? Would she want others to know about the super power or would she keep it secret? If she became a super hero, what would she want her uniform to look like?

DATE:_____ /_____ /_____

❏ *What is one thing that made you mad today?*

WHAT TO EXPECT

This question calls upon each family member to be introspective. One goal of these dinner table conversations is for your children to have an opportunity to see that you as parents are human. Children will benefit from learning that their parents get mad just like they do. Everyone, regardless of age, gets mad or angry at things during the course of a day. If an adult at the table starts this conversation, even young children will share their feelings. Expect to hear about a perceived slight that happened with a friend or classmate, or with a sibling.

Keep the Conversation Going by . . .

Allowing your child to express her anger. How did she feel when she was angry? How did she react? Did she cry? Yell? Keep quiet? What did she do to feel better? How does she feel now? Has the situation been resolved?

DATE:_____ /_____ /_____

❏ *If you had a giant pool and could fill it with anything you wanted, what would you put into the pool?*

WHAT TO EXPECT

This question is apt to elicit the imagination of everyone at the table. Expect to hear imaginative answers from your children of all ages. You may want to give a few suggestions (such as soap bubbles, dolphins, alligators, soup, or other people) to get the ball rolling. Once the conversation starts your children will likely come up with some wild (and improbable) ideas. Just let the talk flow and enjoy it.

Keep the Conversation Going by . . .

Having your child tell you why she would like to have a swimming pool filled with whatever she chose. Would it be fun? Scary? Cool? Gross? What would she do in the pool? Would she still like to swim in it? Who would she invite to share her pool? If she had the choice, would she want just water in her swimming pool? How would she clean it?

DATE:_____ /_____ /_____

❑ *In the next year, what are you looking forward to the most?*

WHAT TO EXPECT

Adults typically think and plan ahead, and they usually
have goals and aspirations. This conversation starter
will prompt your children to gain some maturity by
starting to consider the future. The most common
answers you can expect are things like "my birthday"
or "summer vacation," big milestones that have meaning to children. Since children typically do not plan into
the future, you should be the first one to talk about
what you are looking forward to next year. If appropriate, you can model the idea that what your children
do today impacts what will happen to them tomorrow.

Keep the Conversation Going by . . .

Asking your child why he is looking forward to that
event. How will he feel when it finally occurs? Will
he be excited? Sad? Will he begin looking forward to
something else that is coming up? Does he think that
thing will actually happen next year? Is he going to do
anything to make it more likely that it will happen? If so,
what does he plan to do?

DATE:_____ /_____ /_____

❑ *What is the best thing about our family?*

WHAT TO EXPECT

All of us, even adults, tend to take some of the most important things in our lives for granted. As your children answer this question, expect them to think about the special qualities of a family. This will naturally result in starting to value those unique things about your family. Your children's answers will likely not be highly analytical and will focus on the things that are most important to them, such as the fact that you go to the park together or play cards on Saturday nights. As you and your older family members talk about the things that you value in your family (such as honesty, love, or always supporting each other) they will gain understanding of these important components of family life.

Keep the Conversation Going by . . .

Asking your child why he likes that one thing the best. Does it bring the family closer together? Does he know of other families that are like yours? Does he think that your family adequately expresses and shows your thanks and appreciation for each other and the thing that he likes best?

DATE:_____ /_____ /_____

❑ *Would you rather be a professional basketball player, a famous scientist, or an acclaimed musician?*

WHAT TO EXPECT

This question will prompt your children to think about their potential. The past is the best predictor of the future. A child who is a good athlete probably will want to be a basketball player; a serious student may want to become a scientist, etc. Don't be surprised if your child picks the career that sounds the most exciting or glamorous to him or her at the moment, but which might not have any link to actual talent she has. Children under eleven still see anything as possible.

Keep the Conversation Going by . . .

Encouraging your child to tell you why she would like to be whatever she chose. Does she think she would be good at that? What would be the benefits of becoming her chosen option? What would her life be like? Does she think that would be easy to achieve? Would there be any negatives? Does she think becoming a basketball player/scientist/musician is a possibility? Talk about what you would have chosen at her age.

DATE:_____ /_____ /_____

❑ *If you could give yourself a new name, what name would you choose?*

WHAT TO EXPECT

Children under age seven are likely to choose the name of a friend. Older children might hone in on the name of someone famous or a favorite TV character they perceive as cool. You can be sure all your children will have names at the ready when asked this question since renaming yourself is a common childhood fantasy. The name your child chooses will give you insight into how he sees himself and how he would like to be seen by others.

Keep the Conversation Going by . . .

Asking him why he likes that name. Where has he heard it? Does he think that our names affect our personalities? Would he be a different person if you had named him Rudolf or Sky? What other names does he like? If he had to choose a new last name for your family what would he pick and why?

DATE:_____ /_____ /_____

❑ *Why do you think people want to ban certain books from libraries?*

WHAT TO EXPECT

Start this conversation by explaining what book banning is and give some examples of books that have been banned, such as the Harry Potter series. Expect some initial confusion as your kids wonder why people would want to keep books out of libraries. They may then go to on to say books are banned because they tell lies or say things that hurt people. The older family members at the table can speculate about how a book could harm someone or have information people shouldn't see.

Keep the Conversation Going by . . .

Asking what your child would say to convince someone who did not share that viewpoint. Are there any topics he thinks should be banned from books? Why or why not? Who, if anyone, should be responsible for banning books?

DATE:_____ /_____ /_____

❑ *If you had more money than you would
ever need, with whom would you share
your money or what would you give them?*

WHAT TO EXPECT

This question will guide children toward a sense of social
responsibility. Children eight years old and younger are
likely to give a present to a good friend or to someone
who is likely to give them a gift in return. It is at age ten
that children start to see themselves as young adults. At
this age, children start to gain an understanding of the
inequities in riches and will realize that some people
have a lot, but others have very little. They are apt to
identify a truly needy person and to think about what
gift would be most beneficial.

Keep the Conversation Going by . . .

Encouraging your child to tell you why she would give
a gift to that person (or those people). What does she
think they would do with the money (or things) she
gave them? What would she want them to buy? How
much money does she think she would have if she had
more money than she would ever need?

DATE:_____ /_____ /_____

❑ *We always celebrate birthdays, but we
never celebrate that we are a family. If we
were going to celebrate Family Day, what
would we do?*

WHAT TO EXPECT

Your children will start to think about things the family can do to celebrate Family Day that will be fun for them personally, like getting a bouncy house or going bowling. Your children over eight will latch onto the idea that the day is meant to celebrate family and may suggest things that will encourage involvement by all family members, like a picnic or a game night.

Keep the Conversation Going by . . .

Having your child tell you what celebration Family Day should most resemble. Should it be like Christmas where everyone gives gifts? Should it be like Thanksgiving where the family sits down to eat together? Should you decorate the house? Ask your child if you should invite friends and relatives, or if you should keep the celebration within your family. Is Family Day something your child would really like you to do?

DATE:_____ /_____ /_____

❑ *If someone asked you to create a story about where the sun came from, what story would you make up?*

WHAT TO EXPECT

Being a good storyteller is an art form and there is no better place to hone these skills than over dinner. This question will stir your children's imaginations and stimulate their creativity. Many cultures have a legend to explain the origin of the sun. Our culture even has one. We call it the Big Bang Theory. Barring telling that story (and please don't), the adults at the dinner table are apt to struggle with this question more than the children. We are often held firmly by what we know. Let your children make up their own stories as their imaginations lead them.

Keep the Conversation Going by . . .

Asking your child to keep the story going. What happened after the sun was formed? How does the sun feel about being so hot? Where does the sun go at night? Ask your child to come up with a story about the moon as well.

DATE:_____ /_____ /_____

☐ *Tell us about a time when you surprised yourself at how well you were able to do something.*

WHAT TO EXPECT

It may take a few minutes for any one of your kids to come up with an answer to this one. They will start to remember things they did well. Children under eight will tend to think outside of school and will focus on successfully building a Lego castle, scoring a soccer goal, completing a craft kit, or making cupcakes. Older children may think about academic accomplishments, like a good grade on a test.

Keep the Conversation Going by . . .

Encouraging your child to tell you how she felt when she did a great job. Was she proud of herself? Did she feel a sense of achievement? Does she think that there are other things out there that she can do well, but doesn't yet know about? Talk a bit about a time when you surprised yourself with an accomplishment.

DATE:_____ /_____ /_____

❑ *Sum up your day in ten words or less.*

WHAT TO EXPECT

Your children under eight will blurt out a few quick words like "fun," "stupid," or "boring." Encourage them to try to think of a word for each finger they have. Your older kids will take some time to count off words to make a complete, descriptive sentence. Allow them time to play around and try to fit as much as they can into those ten words.

Keep the Conversation Going by . . .

Implementing a rule that everyone has to say what they want to say in ten words or less during this dinner. This will be hard for some family members—especially if you have one person who is prone to monopolizing the conversation—but it will keep the conversation moving. As you get closer to the end of the meal, you may even want to cut the number of words your family can use down even further. Start by having your child (and the rest of the family) express himself in five words. Then cut down to four, three, two, and maybe even one!

DATE:_____ /_____ /_____

❑ *If you could be a cartoon character, which one would you be?*

WHAT TO EXPECT

Expect your youngest family members to easily and comfortably dominate this conversation, putting you in the role of the listener. The question also requires the adults at the dinner table to talk about being a cartoon character, which temporarily puts them in their children's world, and that is a good thing.

Keep the Conversation Going by . . .

Asking your child to tell you what he likes about his chosen cartoon character. Is the character smart? Funny? Does the character have certain physical traits that your child would want? Can the character survive falls? Does he have the ability to stretch his arms to reach things in high places? How would people respond to your child if he went out of the house looking exactly like his chosen cartoon character?

DATE:_____ /_____ /_____

❑ *If you were put in charge of deciding what big pictures would be hung in your school, what pictures would you put up to make other people feel happy and proud when they saw them?*

WHAT TO EXPECT

This will get your kids thinking about things that are a source of pride or interest to them. They also will think about the kinds of things that make the members of their school community happy. Since the adults at the dinner table best understand the social significance of this question, you should answer it first. Your answer will guide your children towards forming their own answers. The artwork suggested could include murals, paintings, photographs, awards, inspirational posters, favorite artists, or works of community members. Children under eight will initially focus on images that they see in their daily life such as cartoon characters or simple symbols like rainbows or peace signs.

Keep the Conversation Going by . . .

Having your child tell you if her school has any pictures on display that makes her happy or proud when she sees them. What do these pictures look like? What is it about them that makes her happy or proud? Should schools have such pictures? Why? Would your child like to see some of her artwork on display? If so, what would she like to put up on the wall?

DATE:_____ /_____ /_____

❑ *If you could pick one day in your life that you'd like to relive, what day would you pick?*

WHAT TO EXPECT

This is an opportunity for your children to share what is important to them. Expect most of the good days that your children mention to be predictable. A nine-year-old child may mention his or her last birthday party. Someone else may talk about a special Christmas. However, there is a chance that someone will cite a small event that no one else detected. Such comments, if any, will be nuggets of insight.

Keep the Conversation Going by . . .

Letting your child tell you more. What happened that day and why was it so good? Would he want to relive the whole day or just part of it? Did anyone else help make that day so special? Who? Does he think another day like this might happen this year?

DATE: _____ / _____ / _____

❑ *What is the nicest thing anyone ever said to you?*

WHAT TO EXPECT

This conversation starter will allow your children to have the opportunity to share something positive about themselves without feeling like they are boasting or bragging. Alternatively, you will all gain insight into what is important to each other. For younger children, the nicest thing ever said to them will be something within the last few days or several weeks, at best, and could be something superficial.

Keep the Conversation Going by . . .

Asking your child who said that to her. Why does she think they said it? What was your child doing when that person said that to her? Was she hanging out with a friend? Answering a question in class? How did she feel when they said it? Did she say anything back or tell the other person how that compliment made her feel?

DATE:_____ /_____ /_____

❑ *What is the best thing about living in our town or city?*

WHAT TO EXPECT

Expect your children to reflect on the positive things your town or city has to offer them personally, such as a park, playground, or ice cream stand. Everyone in the family will be able to think of something that enriches their lives and your answers will show your children that there are good things about the town or city that they never really thought about.

Keep the Conversation Going by . . .

Asking your child if she thinks your town was always like this. How does she think it got this way? Can she think of something that would make your town even better? Have your child tell you a story about the things she loves about your town.

DATE:_____/_____/_____

❑ *Tell us about a time when you were really afraid.*

WHAT TO EXPECT

Imagined things terrify some children and when they don't share their fears, the fear can take on its own reality. This conversation starter offers you an opportunity to provide a reality check for your child who has been laboring under an imagined fear and for your child to talk about a time when fear was really overpowering. You can expect to hear about common fears, such as being alone in the dark or being outside when lightning struck close.

Keep the Conversation Going by . . .

Encouraging your child to tell you more. Looking back on that time, does it seem now that it was something to be afraid of? Does your child worry that it could happen again? How did he handle his fear? Did he hide? Did he get angry? Does he feel good about the way he handled his fear or does he wish he had done something differently? If he would change the way he handled his fear, what would he do instead?

DATE:_____ /_____ /_____

❑ *What color describes you?*

WHAT TO EXPECT

You might be surprised at how easily your children answer this. Children under seven will probably choose their favorite color and won't analyze what emotion that color is really linked to. If you answer the question and explain how you've chosen a color that is linked to your personality, you'll help them see the way to think about this.

Keep the Conversation Going by . . .

Asking your child why she chose that particular color. Does she think other people see those qualities in her as well? Did she choose her favorite color to represent her? If so, why? What other things does the color that she chose represent? Does your child see those things as being similar to her?

DATE:_____ /_____ /_____

❑ *If you could change one thing about where we live, what would you change?*

WHAT TO EXPECT

Your children will have to think about how where they live affects the quality of their lives. Younger children are apt to think about changes that would directly impact them. So a six-year-old boy might say, "I think we should have a skate park closer to our house." Older children might focus on the weather or distance from friends' houses.

Keep the Conversation Going by . . .

Asking your child if he thinks that many other people would like to see that same change. What would other people in your town or city appreciate about the change? Would the change help adults, other kids, or both? What could your family do to help make that change happen?

DATE:_____ /_____ /_____

❑ *If you had the power to tell everyone in the world one thing they should do and they actually would do it, what would you tell them to do?*

WHAT TO EXPECT

It will take a moment for your children to think this one through. Some of the answers you hear might be a surprise. Even young children have a sense that there are many problems in the world. So a six-year-old might say, "I don't want them to fight." Now it would be hard to argue with that idea. Other children of this age will go with things that are a little lighter, such as "Give out lollipops to all the kids" or "Stand on their heads." Older children will be more contemplative and talk about saying nice things to people or doing things to help people in need.

Keep the Conversation Going by . . .

Asking your child why she would want them to do that. Would it help the world? Would it be funny? Would she have to do it too or would she be able to stand back and watch? Can she see a time when a lot of the people in the world actually did that one thing? Would there be consequences—good or bad—to her request? What would they be and how would she feel about them?

DATE:_____ /_____ /_____

❏ *Why do you think mountain climbers are willing to risk their lives just to climb to the top of a mountain?*

WHAT TO EXPECT

When asked this question, a noted mountain climber replied, "Because it is there." That answer doesn't have much meaning except to another mountain climber. Children under eight might say things like, "Because it's fun." Older children will think about accomplishments and achieving goals, and if they don't, you can guide the conversation in that direction to help everyone understand why someone might do this.

Keep The Conversation Going by . . .

Asking your child if he would like to be a mountain climber. What would he like about it? The freedom? Being out in nature? What would he dislike? The danger? The difficulty? Does he think climbing a mountain would be worth the difficulties he would have to overcome to get to the top? Does he think he would feel a sense of achievement when he reached the top? How would he feel if he started to climb and didn't make it to the top?

DATE: _____ / _____ / _____

❑ *When you have lots of energy, what do you like to do?*

WHAT TO EXPECT

It will be interesting for you to get a sense of how much insight your children have into themselves. Do they accurately recognize when they have lots of energy? Do they make good, well thought out decisions about what to do with that energy? Most children recognize when they have lots of energy, but very few of them are able to constructively channel it; the energy usually takes the child along for the ride. Common answers might include running around outside, playing a sport, or getting silly.

Keep the Conversation Going by . . .

Having your child explain to you why she does what she does when she has extra energy. Does she just try to get it out of her system? Does she use her energy to get something done? If not, what can she do to put her energy to good use? When is having lots of energy a good thing? When is having lots of energy a hard thing?

DATE:_____ /_____ /_____

❑ *What is the best thing for you to do when you get really upset?*

WHAT TO EXPECT

By asking this conversation starter, you will learn two important things: 1) if your children can identify when they are upset, and 2) if your children have a coping mechanism for finding some solace. A surprising number of children do not talk to anyone when they are upset. However, the question has a more important purpose. Developing coping strategies to deal with emotions is a hard-earned skill. Your children will benefit from learning that even adults get upset, but, more importantly, that adults intentionally do things to handle the emotion. With that thought in mind, you should be the first person at the table to answer this question. Children under age eight will likely not focus on the "best" in the question and will simply tell you what they actually do when they are upset, such as cry or yell. Older children will catch this part of the question and give some thought to what is the best way to cope with their emotions and might mention talking to a friend.

Keep the Conversation Going by . . .

Asking your child how she feels when she is upset. Does she feel out of control? Does she just feel angry? Does she talk to anyone when she's upset? Why that person? If she doesn't talk to anyone, why doesn't she? Let your child know that she can always come to you.

DATE:_____ /_____ /_____

❏ *If you had X-ray vision and were in a heli-copter looking down on our house, what would you see?*

WHAT TO EXPECT

You might expect your child to recite exactly what could be seen, but most children will embellish their answer to make it fun and play upon their imagination. Your child might "see" the monsters in the closet or the buried treasure under your house. Have the kids go first and let them inspire you; otherwise they'll prob-ably lose interest while you fret over the leaky pipes the X-ray vision could expose.

Keep the Conversation Going by . . .

Asking your child what would be the weirdest thing that she would see. If it was 2 a.m., do you think they'd see any ghosts? What would they be like? If you were in the house while someone else was looking down with X-ray vision, would there be anything you wouldn't want him or her to see? What would you want to hide and why?

TAKE A TIP:
HOW TO BE A GOOD LISTENER

Listening is the most important part of having good communication and it begins by resisting the temptation to chime in. As soon as you start talking, you stop listening.

Good listeners give the speaker nonverbal feedback that lets her know she is being heard. So, lean slightly forward in your chair, make eye contact, and show facial expressions that mirror the feeling the speaker is conveying. Good listeners are comfortable with silence. They sit quietly while the speaker collects herself or organizes her thoughts. Let the speaker be the first to talk.

Perfect the art of asking open-ended questions, as opposed to closed-ended questions. Closed-ended questions can be answered in a word or two, and those words are usually yes or no. For example, a closed-ended question would be, "Were you scared?" An open-ended question would be, "What did you do then?"

The final and most difficult skill possessed by really good listeners is the art of capturing the speaker's implied but unstated feeling. For example, if the speaker says, "There I was, standing up in front of the entire class and I couldn't remember the next line in the play," and then pauses, a good listener might help the speaker move on by saying, "I suspect you were really embarrassed."

Rely on these tips when you are listening to your child so that he will be encouraged to continue talking with you.

DATE: _____ / _____ / _____

❑ *What would it be like to be an ant that*
lives in the backyard of our house or on
the ground near our home?

WHAT TO EXPECT

When your children are given an opportunity to step
outside of themselves, they often offer some interesting perspectives. If your children who are seven-
years-old and younger go first, they will offer the most
uncensored perspective and report on having to step
over the dog poop, avoid getting hit by the soccer ball,
and scurrying to get out of the way of the big shoes
that come down from the sky. Expect children in the
nine to ten-year-old range to take the question literally.
Older children will turn the question into a joke and
will likely offer some pretty wacky perspectives on the
people who live in the house.

Keep the Conversation Going by . . .

Asking your child what he, as an ant, would think of
the people who live in your home. Would he like them?
Would he fear them? Would they be large? Scary?
Threatening? Would he just ignore them? What would
he see when he saw them? Would he see just their
shoes? Their pant legs? What would it feel like to be
that small?

DATE:_____ /_____ /_____

☐ *What do you do when someone you care about is very sad?*

WHAT TO EXPECT

Many children have not thought much about what they would do to cheer up someone who is sad, so expect a few moments of silence as everyone thinks. This conversation starter should increase your children's commitment to be intentional about doing something that will cheer up someone who is sad. Younger children will suggest something that would make themselves feel better, such as giving the person a hug or giving him or her a gift.

Keep the Conversation Going by . . .

Asking your child if she recalls a time when someone was sad and she tried to help the person feel better. What did she do? Does she recall a time when she was sad and someone did something to make her feel better? What did that person do? Would she do the same for someone else?

DATE:_____ /_____ /_____

❑ *What is one thing that our family does that is different than most families?*

WHAT TO EXPECT

As your children answer this question, they will think about what makes your family unique and special and that will enhance the pride they feel about it. Children under eight may not have much experience with how other families function but if you suggest they compare your family to another family (such as a close friend's or a cousin's) they will be able to see some differences.

Keep the Conversation Going by . . .

Asking your child if she likes the fact that your family is different. Is it a good thing or a bad thing? What is fun about being different? Would your child like to do more of the things that set your family apart? If the answer is yes, ask, "What can you do to help that happen?"

DATE:_____ /_____ /_____

❏ *If you were asked to be the lead role in a movie, what would you want that movie to be about?*

WHAT TO EXPECT
Expect your children to describe a movie that is similar to one they have recently seen and particularly enjoyed. They may also make up a subject for a movie based on something they read or saw elsewhere, such as in a book or at school. Commonly, kids will describe a movie that will allow them to play the role of a character they like or admire. The character they select will give you insight into their value system. Older children are apt to describe a movie with a more detailed plot that incorporates special effects.

Keep the Conversation Going by . . .
Asking your child why he described that type of movie. Where would this movie take place? What other characters would be in the movie? How does the movie end?

DATE: _____ / _____ / _____

☐ *If someone gave you a frog and told you that it could be trained to do anything that you needed help with, what would you train it to do?*

WHAT TO EXPECT

For most children, it is easier for them to talk through something like a puppet than it is for them to own their own thoughts and feelings. So this question makes it easy for your children to discuss something that has been causing them difficulty. Your child could say the frog could be trained to do her homework or her household chores. Listen for any revealing statements, such as "Jump in the mouth of anyone who says something mean to me," which reveals an ongoing issue or concern.

Keep the Conversation Going by . . .

Asking your child to tell you how she's going to train the frog. How will she teach him how to do the thing that she wants him to do? What will it be like to watch the frog help her out? What color will the frog be? Pink? Black? What will it look like? What is your child going to give the frog in return for helping her out? How might the frog feel about all of this?

DATE:_____/_____/_____

☐ *If company were coming to visit and stay with us for several days, what one thing in our town would you want to show them?*

WHAT TO EXPECT

This question will enhance the pride that your children feel about their community. Expect your children to identify places to have fun, like the water park, the playground where there are swings, or the swimming pool. Adults at the table will likely mention cultural events, historic places, or good restaurants.

Keep the Conversation Going by . . .

Asking your child why he would want to show someone from out of town that particular thing. Is it his favorite thing in town? Why? Does he think your visitor will have fun there too? Will the visitor have seen something like that before? Do other towns have something like that, or is that unique to your town?

DATE: _____ / _____ / _____

❑ *How could your family be greener?*

WHAT TO EXPECT

Children of all ages are familiar with the idea of becoming more environmentally friendly, so your children have already heard the concept at school and on TV. Children who are between five and seven will likely share ideas they have learned at school, such as recycling paper, turning off the water faucet, and turning off the lights. Older children will suggest ideas based on things your family does and might offer ideas like walking to the store instead of driving or riding the bus or closing doors to keep in heat or air conditioning. Talking about this concept will help your children become environmentally aware on a personal level.

Keep the Conversation Going by . . .

Finding out what your child does at school to be green. Why is it important for her to try to be green? What will it do for your family and for the planet? What happens to things that are recycled? What can your child do to remember to be green on a regular basis?

DATE:_____ /_____ /_____

❑ *What would you do if you had a snow day and school was cancelled?*

WHAT TO EXPECT

In busy families, there often isn't much down time to just enjoy each other and enjoy favorite activities. This topic will give your children time to think about what they would do with the windfall of a free day. Expect to hear the wish list of what your kids have been thinking about but haven't had time to fit in, such as sleeping late, watching movies, playing games, making a favorite recipe, or even playing in the snow!

Keep the Conversation Going by . . .

Asking your child if she would want to invite someone over to enjoy the snow day with her. Why would she invite that person? Would she do something different if that friend was there than if she was alone? If so, why? What did she do the last time she suddenly and unexpectedly had a free day?

DATE: _____ / _____ / _____

❑ *What would you do for fun if the television were broken for a week?*

WHAT TO EXPECT

Expect this question to get your children thinking about less sedentary and more interactive activities, but they may need to think for a while to come up with ideas. The resultant conversation may renew interest in a favorite board game, card game, or activity outside the house. As they talk more about it, they may realize that in fact there are lots of things they can do that don't involve the TV.

Keep the Conversation Going by . . .

Having your child think about having a no TV night. Would he be interested in turning off the TV one day a week and doing some of the fun activities that were brought up? How might it be more fun to interact with the family than sitting in front of the TV? What are the advantages? Are there any disadvantages he can think of?

DATE:_____ /_____ /_____

❑ *If you could be a vehicle, what would you be?*

WHAT TO EXPECT

When you open up this question to include any vehicle, you'll hear some varied answers from your kids. Your son might want to be a fire truck, with its flashing lights and sirens. Your daughter might suggest that being an ice cream truck would be the most fun. Children will choose something that appeals to their interests and what they perceive as suiting their personality. Children over age nine, in particular boys, might have a favorite sports car they would want to be. Jump into the conversation and talk about what you would be—maybe you would want to be an ambulance or an airplane.

Keep the Conversation Going by . . .

Encouraging your child to tell you where she would like to go if she was a vehicle. What would be the best place for her type of vehicle to do its job? Why did she choose that particular kind of transportation? Who would be driving her? Would she go fast or slow?

129

DATE: _____ / _____ / _____

❑ *If you heard someone making fun of your friend, what would you do?*

WHAT TO EXPECT

This has happened to or will happen to everyone at some point. Talking about this as a family will give your children a chance to think about how they have handled this in the past and how they would like to handle it in the future. Expect to hear a wide variety of responses ranging from listening and doing nothing, to walking away, to intervening with a comment in defense of a friend, or agreeing with the speaker.

Keep the Conversation Going by . . .

Asking your child why he would react that way. What does he think the result would be if he did that? What would he want his friends to do if someone was talking about him? How would he feel if they did nothing? If you have ever been in this situation, tell your child what you did and how you felt when you were on the other side of things.

DATE:_____ /_____ /_____

❑ *How would you describe yourself to someone who doesn't know you yet?*

WHAT TO EXPECT

This question will get your children to think about how they come across to others. However, awareness of oneself develops over time and is highly influenced by hearing what others say about you. Since young children may have a difficult time with this question, the adults at the dinner table should go first. Even then, you may be tempted to finish your child's sentences. Don't. Let each child get his story out.

Keep the Conversation Going by . . .

Asking your child if the person he described himself to would be surprised by how he actually is upon meeting him. How does he think his best friend would describe him? How would your child describe the other members of your family to someone who hadn't met them yet?

DATE:_____ /_____ /_____

❑ *What could you do to cheer up a friend who is recovering after being sick for a whole week?*

WHAT TO EXPECT

Most families value a sense of loyalty to friends and social responsibility to help others in need. This conversation starter will begin that discussion in a concrete way. Young children may think about sharing a stuffed animal, toy, or a comfort object such as a blanket. Older children may think of calling their friend or making a get-well card. You could share stories of visiting a friend in the hospital or making a meal for a family while they attend to a loved one.

Keep the Conversation Going by . . .

Having your child tell you how her suggestion would help cheer up her friend. Would she like it if someone did that for her if she was sick? What is the first thing she would do with her friend when her friend was well enough to play or hang out?

DATE: _____ / _____ / _____

❑ *What is the best Halloween costume you have ever seen?*

WHAT TO EXPECT

This conversation will provide many opportunities to teach your children how to use descriptive words. Use this conversation starter as an opportunity to enhance and expand their use of adjectives of like scary, weird, wacky, cute, funny, comical, peculiar, strange, spectacular, and amazing. Children under eight will likely refer to a costume they recently saw or recall from their last Halloween. Expect them to choose costumes they would enjoy wearing.

Keep the Conversation Going by . . .

Asking your child who was wearing that costume. What did other people think of the costume? What color was the costume? Does your child think the costume came from a store or was homemade? What exactly does your child like about the costume? Would he like to wear that costume next Halloween? If he were to make one change to the costume, what would he change? Why? Would he change something he didn't like or add something to the costume to make it even more over-the-top?

DATE: _____ / _____ / _____

❑ *If you wanted to catch a skunk without getting sprayed, how would you do it?*

WHAT TO EXPECT

Start this conversation by asking the question to the youngest child at the dinner table. She is apt to use food to entice the skunk into a box and then shut the door, which is pretty clever. From there, the answers will get more inventive and could involve nets, tranquilizer guns, or traps. A ten-year-old might want to catch the skunk by building a covered pit where the skunk usually walks.

Keep the Conversation Going by . . .

Asking your child if he has ever smelled a skunk. Does he know anyone who got sprayed or does he know of anybody's dog that got sprayed by a skunk? Why does he think skunks spray? Why does he think it smells so bad? If skunks didn't spray, would they be cute animals? What kinds of things do other animals do to protect themselves?

DATE:_____ /_____ /_____

❑ *If you could ask your favorite singer/song-writer two questions, what would you ask?*

WHAT TO EXPECT

Expect your children to want to know what inspired the musician to write the song, if a song was written for a particular person, or how long it took to write the song. Older family members may be curious about how a singer chose a particular song or how difficult it was to record the song. There may even be interest in following up with some Internet research to find the answers to the family questions. Feel free to link this conversation starter to another family activity that is musical in nature or to a TV show singing contest which has exposed your children to young aspiring singers and songwriters.

Keep the Conversation Going by . . .

Asking your child if she would be nervous talking to her favorite singer or songwriter. If so, why? What does she think it is like to be a professional singer? Are there pressures that she would have to deal with? Would she like to be a popular singer or songwriter? How would she feel about having fans?

DATE:_____ /_____ /_____

❑ *The weekend will soon be here. What are you looking forward to doing?*

WHAT TO EXPECT

Expect to find that your children probably haven't thought about what they want to do with the weekend, and that is the point of the question. Learning to make the most of time is a slowly acquired skill, and you can help your children cultivate the practice. Suggest that your child think about what he did last weekend and then use those ideas to come up some things to do this weekend. Are there things he enjoys doing that he has not had time for lately?

Keep the Conversation Going by . . .

Asking your child to tell you more about what she could do over the weekend. Is she excited about the plan she came up with? Who will she do that with? What type of preparation will that plan require? Will she need your help to put the plan into action?

DATE:_____ /_____ /_____

❑ *Neil Armstrong was the first man to walk on the moon. As he made his first step, he said, "One small step for man. One giant leap for mankind." Obviously, he prepared those remarks in advance. If you were the first person to walk on Mars, what would you say?*

WHAT TO EXPECT

Kids will need to think about this for a minute, but you can expect some off the cuff answers about saying hello to Martians and versions of Armstrong's quote. As they think about it more, they will offer some thoughtful answers and may make some silly comments as well. Have them focus on how historic the moment would be and how they would feel.

Keep the Conversation Going by . . .

Asking your child if he would prepare something in advance like Armstrong did or if he would say something in the moment. If Neil Armstrong had not given his well-prepared remarks, what does your child think he would have said? How would your child feel if he had the opportunity to walk on Mars? Scared? Excited? Nervous? Tell him how you would feel.

DATE:_____ /_____ /_____

❑ *Would you rather ride on a horse, an elephant, or a camel?*

WHAT TO EXPECT

Expect this conversation starter to appeal to your children's sense of adventure. You might well hear some excitement and an animated conversation from your children. Most children will be enticed at the idea of riding the more exotic of these animals, but if you have a horse lover in the house you can probably predict the answer you'll get!

Keep the Conversation Going by . . .

Having your child tell you why she would choose to ride that particular animal. Where would she go on that animal? How does she think the ride would feel? Would it be bumpy? Slow? Awkward? Fast? Fun? Exciting? Would the animal have a saddle or would she ride bareback? What would she hold on to? What would the animal's name be? How would the animal feel if she petted it?

DATE:_____/_____/_____

❏ *If you were giving a news report about your family, what would you say?*

WHAT TO EXPECT

Young children will focus on events that have happened in the last day or two and will emphasize activities or events that impacted them the most. Children over age eight will have a longer look back period to reflect on. Answering this question will help your child process events and reframe them in terms of importance. You might also get some funny stories that poke fun at you or your child's siblings.

Keep the Conversation Going by . . .

Asking your child what he would include for sports, weather, or entertainment news. Encourage your children to tell the news in a way that sounds like a news broadcast. What kinds of news do you usually share with each other? Who else might be interested in hearing your family's news broadcast?

DATE:_____ /_____ /_____

❑ *Would you rather ride in a submarine, a hot air balloon, or a glider?*

WHAT TO EXPECT

This conversation starter will let you get a sense of each child's awareness of unconventional modes of transportation. For example, a young child may ask, "What is a glider?" There will be a brief period of silence as the children imagine what it would be like to be in each of these conveyances. Then the flood gate will open . . .

Keep the Conversation Going by . . .

Having your child explain why he chose the mode he did. Why that one? Is he more interested in underwater adventures? Is he afraid of heights? Where did he learn about that particular type of machine? Where would he go in that machine? Who would he take with him?

DATE:_____ /_____ /_____

❑ *Why do you think roosters crow when the sun comes up in the morning?*

WHAT TO EXPECT

Expect your children to put on their thinking caps for this one. Younger children will have simplistic answers, like "To tell everyone to wake up." It's unlikely anyone at your table will know why roosters do this, so you can brainstorm together and evaluate possible reasons.

Keep the Conversation Going by . . .

Having your child think about the question more deeply. Does she think roosters really do crow when the sun comes up? If it was six in the morning, but the sun was hidden behind heavy clouds, would the rooster still crow? What time does the rooster have to get up in the morning if he crows when the sun comes up? Would your child like to be the one to wake up the rooster? How would she wake the rooster up?

DATE:_____ /_____ /_____

❑ *What was the worst thing that ever happened to you in school?*

WHAT TO EXPECT

Almost everyone has had a terrible thing happen in school. Sometimes the worst things were comments or experiences that forever killed aspirations and self-confidence. Parents need to know if their children have experienced a potentially devastating comment or experience so that they can try to remedy it. You can expect that your children will have at least one bad experience to share. Oftentimes, you will hear about a foolish comment made by a teacher or a punishment that your child felt was undeserved. Other common responses involve being made fun of by other children.

Keep the Conversation Going by . . .

Encouraging your child to tell you about the bad things that happen at school. Ask her if the bad thing she told you about still bothers her. Does she know why it happened? Does she know if anything like that happened to other children? Does she think something like that could happen again?

DATE:_____ /_____ /_____

❑ *Think of your favorite movie. Now imag-*
ine that you're in charge of making a new
version of that movie. What would you do
to make it even better?

WHAT TO EXPECT

Expect this question to get your children talking about
their taste in movies, which probably will all be quite
different. Children six and under will like movies with
cartoon characters. Boys seven to eleven will like movies
that depict power and dominance. Girls may be more
interested in movies about relationships such as friendships and simple romances. More importantly, each child
will get an opportunity to think about putting his or her
personal touch on a movie.

Keep the Conversation Going by . . .

Asking your child to give you specifics about what
changes she would make. What scenes would she add?
Would she take any one character out of her new version of the movie? Would she add an additional character? What would that character be like? Who would
play that character? Would she change the ending? How
does she think audiences would respond to her version?

143

DATE: _____ / _____ / _____

❑ *What animal are you most like?*

WHAT TO EXPECT

We attribute distinct qualities to many animals. Foxes are cunning. Cats are independent. Cows are stupid. The animal that your child selects will give you insight into the qualities he or she admires and wishes to emulate. Children six and younger are apt to pick cartoon-like characters such as Big Bird. Children seven to ten will likely select exotic animals, ones they have seen on nature programs, like a polar bear. Children eleven and older are apt to pick an animal based on its distinctive qualities.

Keep the Conversation Going by . . .

Encouraging your child to tell you more about her choice. Why did she choose that animal? What qualities does that animal have that she likes or that she relates to? Does she like how that animal looks? If she were that animal, how would she spend her day?

DATE:_____ /_____ /_____

❑ *Name one thing you would do to help the earth be a better place to live.*

WHAT TO EXPECT

This question should stimulate each child's sense of social responsibility. Children ten and younger might select some grand action like giving everyone a nice house or a new car. Older children will see the depth of the question and will think of small things that they might realistically do such as recycling waste materials or conserving energy.

Keep the Conversation Going by . . .

Encouraging your child to tell you more about his choice. Why would doing that be important to him? Why does he think helping the earth is a good thing? Can he tell you about any of the environmental problems the earth is facing right now? Does he know of anyone trying to do something like that? What might he do to make that wish happen?

DATE:_____ /_____ /_____

❑ *What chore do you dislike doing the most and why?*

WHAT TO EXPECT

Expect everyone to have some chore such as making the bed, picking up their things, or putting away the dishes that they dislike doing. But by thinking about and discussing the household chores, family members will be more aware of how everyone contributes to efficient functioning of the house.

Keep the Conversation Going by . . .

Asking your child to tell you more about why she hates the chore that she hates. Is it messy? Does it take too much time? Does she understand why the chore needs to be done? What would happen if no one did that particular chore? If she could pick anyone to do the chore for her, who would she pick? What chore would she do for them in exchange?

DATE:_____ /_____ /_____

❑ *If you had to fight to free someone you care about from an evil dragon, how would you defeat the dragon?*

WHAT TO EXPECT

This question empowers children to think of themselves as invincible and heroic. Children under seven are likely to invoke magic or use methods that might make you scratch your head, while older children will think up strategies that are better thought out. Encouraging children to think about dealing with danger in a safe scenario like this one helps them feel more confident about dealing with real life problems.

Keep the Conversation Going by . . .

Finding out what kind of help your child might need to defeat the dragon. Who would she call? Would she have to kill the dragon or is there another solution? How would she feel while fighting the dragon? How would she feel when she is victorious?

DATE: _____ / _____ / _____

❑ *What would be the coolest thing about being an airplane pilot?*

WHAT TO EXPECT

This conversation starter will help expand your children's sense of what is possible and what they could be. It will also help you find out if your child is a risk taker. Some children will say, "Nothing. I wouldn't like to be a pilot." Another child might say, "I would love to fly upside down under a bridge."

Keep the Conversation Going by . . .

Having your child tell you what some of the perks of being a pilot could be. Would she have a great view of her city? Would she have someone bring her dinner in the cockpit? Does she think she might want to be an airplane pilot someday? How much training does she think she would have to have?

DATE:_____ /_____ /_____

❑ *What do you think it would be like to have special problems or challenges, such as a physical handicap or a mental disability?*

WHAT TO EXPECT

Children under eight may not understand the concept of a disability, and it will have to be explained to them. Once they can picture what it might be like to be blind or to not be able to walk, they will formulate some basic scenarios that would impact things they care the most about, such as you couldn't watch TV if you were blind or you couldn't play soccer if your legs didn't work. Older children will be able to understand the disability better and will have seen how some people cope, so they may point out that a person in a wheelchair wouldn't be able to reach the kitchen counter to cook or a person who is missing both arms wouldn't be able to drive a car.

Keep the Conversation Going by . . .

Asking your child if he knows anyone who has a special problem or disability. If he does know someone, ask him how he thinks that person is affected by that disability. Suggest that your child put himself in that person's shoes for a while. For example, if the person is blind, have your child take a shower with his eyes closed. If your child doesn't know anyone with a disability, have him give more detail about how he thinks a disability could affect someone.

DATE:_____ /_____ /_____

❑ *The Lakota are an Indian tribe who see power in animals. If you were a Lakota, what power would you see in a hawk?*

WHAT TO EXPECT

The Lakota traditionally believe that the hawk is the source of swiftness in action and inner stamina. What your child thinks is the hawk's power will depend on what he sees in his mind's eye as he visualizes a hawk circling in search of food. Some might see sharp, keen vision. A few might think of the hawk's patience—waiting and waiting to find a mouse. Others might see what the Lakota see—the swiftness of the strike or the stamina to circle for hour after hour.

Keep the Conversation Going by . . .

Asking your child to think about the things that hawks do better than almost any other animal. How would having that power or those skills help him in his life? What might he do to have some of the hawk's power?

DATE:_____ /_____ /_____

❑ *When you get a place of your own, what kind of pet do you want to have?*

WHAT TO EXPECT

Childhood does not last forever. It will be useful for children to start thinking about what their lives will be like when they become young adults. You can expect a wide range of answers, and some of them will be impractical. For example a child who is now six-years-old may say, "When I get a house, I'm going to get a horse." Don't ask him where he is going to keep his horse. He will, of course, keep it in his bedroom.

Keep the Conversation Going by . . .

Encouraging your child to tell you more about his pet. Where will the pet sleep? What will his name be? What will he eat? When will your child feed him? Is your child going to have any other pets? If so, what kinds of animals will those pets be? What will their names be? Will all the pets in house get along? What will your child do if they don't?

DATE:_____ /_____ /_____

❑ *If our family was to form a band, but all of our instruments had to be things found in the house or the garage, what could we come up with for instruments?*

WHAT TO EXPECT

You'll get some obvious answers first, such as pots and pans as drums and wind chimes for bells. As your children think more, they will come up with some creative ideas, such as filling containers with beans for maracas or using chains to make music. They will begin to see the potential for musical sound in almost everything in your home.

Keep the Conversation Going by . . .

Moving into a discussion about music. What types of music would your child like to play on these homemade instruments? Is there a real instrument she would actually like to learn how to play? After dinner, everyone could try making music with the instruments they have suggested.

DATE:_____ /_____ /_____

❑ *If you could design your own clothes,*
what would they look like?

WHAT TO EXPECT

This discussion will help your children realize that what
they wear and how they look has an impact on other
people. Children under age eight will probably first
base their imaginary outfit on clothes they like, such
as super hero outfits or clothes that depict a favorite
character (such as Barbie or SpongeBob). As they think
about it though, they will get more imaginative and
may come up with outfits that have built-in wings, TV
screens, or jewels. Older children will focus on outfits
they have seen other children wearing and which signify
their desire to fit in.

Keep the Conversation Going by . . .

Asking your child where she will go when wearing that
outfit. Does she have a specific destination in mind?
Does she think other people will like her outfit? Will
they want to wear something similar? Will she acces-
sorize the outfit with jewelry or a hat? Will those items
be important to the look she is trying to create? If your
child had to create an outfit for you, what would it look
like? Be sure to talk about an outfit you would create
for yourself as well.

DATE: _____ / _____ / _____

☐ *Why do you like going to a big playground or a park?*

WHAT TO EXPECT

Expect your children to focus on the activities they like at the park, such as swinging, going down the slide, playing in the the sand box, or playing on the teeter totter. This conversation will give you some insight into the physical activities your kids enjoy. Your children might also mention that they enjoy playing with the other kids who are there, or spending time with you when you push them on the swings.

Keep the Conversation Going by . . .

Asking your child about the last time he went to a park or playground. Who took him there? Did he bring a friend with him? What did he do there? What was his favorite thing to do? If he could bring anything home from the park or playground, what would he bring and what would he do with it?

DATE:_____ /_____ /_____

❑ *What makes you feel better when you are sick?*

WHAT TO EXPECT

Since we generally feel better when someone does something for us, this question will help your children realize that others in the family do a lot for them, especially at critical times. Your children might say something like, "a cool towel on my forehead," "ice cream for a sore throat," "sipping soup," or "crawling into bed and resting."

Keep the Conversation Going by . . .

Having your child tell the table about the time she felt the sickest. How did she feel? Who took care of her? Did anyone do any of the things she mentioned for her then? How would she take care of someone else who didn't feel well?

DATE:_____ /_____ /_____

☐ *Out of all of the things you are good at,*
what is the one thing that you do the
best?

WHAT TO EXPECT

This is a chance to brag, and a little bit of bragging to encouraging ears is a good thing. Your children will reflect on their skills and abilities and suggest the one thing that they do the best. Expect them to reflect specifically on the things that they enjoy doing. They might say "I'm good at running," "I'm best at drawing," or "I can do math."

Keep the Conversation Going by . . .

Asking your child how he feels when he does that one thing. Smart? Capable? Proud? How did he acquire that ability? Does he know anyone else who is good at that thing as well? How does he put that ability to its best use?

DATE:_____ /_____ /_____

❏ *If you had to choose a nickname for yourself, what would it be?*

WHAT TO EXPECT

You can expect a surprise or two. One of your children is apt to suggest a nickname that no one would have guessed that he or she would like. Family members are apt to gain insight into something that is important to another member of the family, but had not been previously disclosed. It also offers an opportunity for you to make yourself more human in your children's eyes by telling them what your nickname used to be or what you would like your nickname to be now.

Keep the Conversation Going by . . .

Asking your child why he would choose that nickname. Has anyone called him by that nickname? Does it have special meaning to him? If he could give someone else in your family a nickname, who would he choose and what would that nickname be? What does he think about nicknames in general? Why have a nickname? Is it cool? Is it fun? Is it funny?

DATE:_____ /_____ /_____

❑ *If you could build a town underground, what would it look like?*

WHAT TO EXPECT
This question will stimulate creative and imaginative thinking. Young children may have seen an ant farm and could build upon this experience. Older children may have read the story of Peter Pan and the lost boys who lived imaginatively under a tree. This is another question that probably will be easier for children to answer than for adults because it requires setting aside the conventional.

Keep the Conversation Going by . . .
Asking your child to describe how things would work in the town. Would the town have electricity? Running water? Where would it come from? Would your child like living there? Why? Would there be any advantages to living underground? Any disadvantages?

DATE:_____ /_____ /_____

❑ *What is something you have been think-ing about today, but haven't shared with anyone?*

WHAT TO EXPECT

Through this conversation, your children will get an opportunity to experience, even in a small dose, the relief that comes from sharing thoughts. The thoughts that children don't share are typically things that trouble or worry them. If your child is reluctant to answer this question, you can start by answering it yourself. Tell your child it could be something small, such as how he thought the hamburgers at lunch were really good, or something that has to do with how a certain person made him feel. Once everyone starts sharing things, everyone will loosen up and share deeper thoughts.

Keep the Conversation Going by . . .

Asking your child to tell you how he feels after talking about something he has been holding inside. Does he feel relieved? Comforted? Did talking about what he has been thinking about give him any ideas? Does he feel that he can talk about anything whenever he wants?

DATE:_____ /_____ /_____

❑ *If you were going to give someone a birthday present, but all you had was a box of crayons, a paper bag, and colored yarn, what would you make?*

WHAT TO EXPECT

This exercise will allow your children to think about creating a birthday greeting for someone special. Sometimes the best birthday presents are handmade and it is the thought that counts! Your children might first think of making a card, but may move to the idea of a puppet, a freeform sculpture, or even a necklace.

Keep the Conversation Going by . . .

Asking your child who she would give the present to. Does she think that person would be surprised by the gift? How would the gift be wrapped? In regular wrapping paper? Would it even need to be wrapped? What would your child like to receive if someone was making a gift for her out of the same materials?

DATE:_____ /_____ /_____

❑ *What is your favorite word and why?*

WHAT TO EXPECT

This question provides an opportunity for some fun word play around your table. Your children will enjoy picking the funniest and silliest sounding words they can come up with. As the teens and adults at the table chime in with some serious choices, kids may analyze the question in that way as well and offer some serious choices of their own. If they stick with silliness though, just roll with it.

Keep the Conversation Going by . . .

Asking your child why she chose the word. What is the longest word she knows? What is the happiest sounding word she can think of? Is there a word that makes her feel unhappy? Are there words she uses very often? What are they? Are there words she has heard but doesn't know the meaning of?

DATE: _____ / _____ / _____

❑ *You have been selected to go establish a town on Mars. What will your town be like?*

WHAT TO EXPECT

Expect your children to weigh the issues of survival with the question of values—each at their own level of understanding. Children nine and younger will likely build a town with parks that have swings and swimming pools. Older children will think about the harsh climate on Mars as they design their town.

Keep the Conversation Going by . . .

Asking your child if he would like his town on Mars to be similar to your town now. What characteristics of where you live now would he want to include in the new town? Who would he want to help him establish a town on Mars? Why would he choose that person or those people? What unique challenges will your child face when designing his town? Will he have to make sure oxygen is pumped in or that people wear space-suits to protect themselves from the heat?

DATE:_____ /_____ /_____

❏ *What would your life be like if you could read people's minds?*

WHAT TO EXPECT

Your children will hit upon the easiest and most beneficial answers first—they would know the answers to tests and they would know what they're getting for Christmas. As you talk about the concept in depth, they may realize they would never have a surprise again and would always know when people were lying. This conversation gives them insight into the importance of privacy when it comes to thoughts.

Keep the Conversation Going by . . .

Finding out if he would tell anyone he had this ability. What would the disadvantages be to knowing everyone's thoughts? How would she feel if someone could read her mind? How different would the world be if we could read everyone's thoughts?

DATE:_____ /_____ /_____

❑ *If you were to dye your hair, what color would you dye it?*

WHAT TO EXPECT

This question will make it easy for everyone in the family to talk on an equal basis. Your children will likely go for colors that have shock value. Purple and lime green are definitely not out of the question! This question allows your children to fantasize about radical appearance changes they would likely never really try.

Keep the Conversation Going by . . .

Asking your child why she would choose that color out of all the colors out there. What would that color say about her? Does pink show that she's a girly girl? Does black show that she's dark? Does red show that she's fiery? Does she know anyone who colors his or her hair? What reasons can she think of for dyeing one's hair? Be sure to jump in and offer your own opinion about this question.

DATE:_____ /_____ /_____

❑ *If you wrote a book about your life, what is one story about yourself that would absolutely have to be in the book?*

WHAT TO EXPECT

Expect everyone at your table to have a story. Your kids are likely to choose stories that have to do with exciting events, such as birthdays or parties, or very significant moments within their own world view, such as the day you got a dog. This question is also an opportunity for you to engage in the type of self-disclosure that makes you more human and approachable to your children. Family bonds will be built with the sharing of such personal information.

Keep the Conversation Going by . . .

Asking your child why that particular story needs to end up in the book. Is it is a funny story? A sad story? Did he learn a lesson that he wants to teach others? How old was he when that happened? Has he ever told anyone that story? Are there other stories that would definitely be in the book? Would the book be different if someone else at the table wrote it about him?

DATE:_____ /_____ /_____

❑ *If I could have traveled in your backpack today, what interesting things would I have seen and what would I have heard?*

WHAT TO EXPECT

Expect each child to reflect on his or her day. This conversation starter may present an opportunity to help them bridge the connection between what happened to them—good or bad—and what they might have done to at least contribute to the situation. What you will hear will depend in part on whether that child is inherently an optimist or pessimist. The optimist will report the good things that happened. The pessimist will report the negative things that happened.

Keep the Conversation Going by . . .

Encouraging your child to tell you more. Was what happened today a surprise to your child when it happened? Why does she think that happened? Would she have done things differently if she had known you would be in her backpack? What does she think it would be like to have spent the day in your purse or briefcase?

DATE: _____ / _____ / _____

❑ *What tall tale have you heard that you once believed but are now starting to think might not really be true? For example, do you think that Jack really climbed up a bean stalk?*

WHAT TO EXPECT

Nearly everyone has believed at least one story that is not true. Perhaps to stretch children's imaginations, adults tell children lots of things that are patently false and then simply allow for children to find out on their own that they are untrue. The adults at the dinner table will reflect on their youth and laugh as they recount things they once swallowed hook, line, and sinker. Teenagers might do the same. Your children who are over ten may pipe up (or want to pipe up) about things like Santa Claus or the tooth fairy, so be ready to stop them if you don't want your younger children to hear this. Younger children will probably share about times someone told them something silly that wasn't true—like the time Uncle Jack pretended that he was raised in the jungle.

Keep the Conversation Going by . . .

Having your child tell you how she found out that the story or tale was not true. Did someone at school tell her? Was there something about the story that didn't sound right? Can she make up a story that someone might believe at first, but later on realize that it wasn't true?

DATE:_____ /_____ /_____

❑ *What is the bravest thing you ever saw anyone do?*

WHAT TO EXPECT

Most of us go for long periods of time without seeing acts of bravery or even situations that warrant an act of bravery. Because they want to immediately contribute to the conversation, your children could exaggerate or even invent an act of bravery they witnessed. Accept it at face value. They simply want to be part of the conversation. You can help them think of real acts of bravery by pointing out the everyday bravery that goes on around us—firemen rescuing people, children getting through a vaccination, people going into a dark room when they are afraid of the dark, and more.

Keep the Conversation Going by . . .

Asking your child if he thinks the person was scared when he/she was doing it? Were they scared afterward? Why does he think the person did it? Have your child talk about brave things he's seen on TV, such as skydiving or deep sea diving.

DATE: _____ / _____ / _____

❑ *If a genie granted you an extra day this week, how would you spend it?*

WHAT TO EXPECT

Expect your children to see this extra day as an opportunity to have fun. They will want to go swimming, skate boarding, or some such thing. They will likely envision the day as a free day and won't think about chores or what it might mean to have an extra day of school to go to! Older kids are more likely to use the extra day to hang out with their friends.

Keep the Conversation Going by . . .

Having your child tell you why she wants to do the things she chose. Why does she not feel she has enough time during the week to do them? If the genie does not give her this extra day, will she be able to find the time to do these things? How important is it for her to do these things? If she could ask the genie for another wish, what would she wish for?

DATE:_____ /_____ /_____

☐ *Would you rather live in a big city, a small town, or in the country?*

WHAT TO EXPECT

This conversation starter will allow you to learn about the lifestyle that most appeals to each of your children. It will be interesting and important to find out if there are any intensely felt differences or preferences. Expect your children to want to live someplace other than where they are living, while adults in the family will probably prefer to live right where they are.

Keep the Conversation Going by . . .

Having your child tell you why she would like to live there. What are some things she would like to do there? How does she feel about the two options that she didn't choose? What are the disadvantages to living in those places? Where would she live in the place she did choose? A house? An apartment? A tent?

DATE:_____ /_____ /_____

❑ *Carefully select a problem sent to an advice column like Ann Landers or Dear Abby (friendship questions are particularly appropriate). Read the question, but not the answer. Ask your child, "What advice would you give?"*

WHAT TO EXPECT

The advice is apt to vary widely from one child to another, providing a spark to your dinner conversation. Also, your children's skills at understanding interpersonal problems will be enhanced as they listen to the adults at the table weigh in with their advice. Start with the younger members of the family. They are apt to have some unique answers. Their advice may be simple, yet elegant, such as "She should just tell the truth."

Keep the Conversation Going by . . .

Asking your child why he thinks that solution will work. How would he feel if he were in that person's place? Has he ever been in that person's place? If he were to write in with a problem, what would that problem be? How would he want readers to respond to his question?

DATE:_____ /_____ /_____

❑ *If you could add one thing of any size to our home or yard that would make this a better home, what would it be?*

WHAT TO EXPECT

Expect each child to have something unique to suggest. Your children are likely to come up with things that speak to an interest of theirs, such as a pool, basketball court, horse barn, dance studio, or hockey rink. Younger children may focus on toys such as bikes, swing sets, or bouncy houses. It will be interesting to discover whether any of your family members would like the same thing.

Keep the Conversation Going by . . .

Encouraging your child to tell you how that addition would make your home better. What would it add? Would it be something fun? Would it be big or small? Why does she want it? What would it take for her to add that to your home? If your child can't have that, what is something along that line that you may be able to give her? For example, if a swimming pool is unrealistic, what about a plastic wading pool?

DATE:_____ /_____ /_____

❑ *What does love mean to you?*

WHAT TO EXPECT
Most of us take love for granted, if not all of the time, at least part of the time. This question will help children focus on a deeper understanding of what love is and how it affects us. Expect answers that are very simple—such as "a hug," or "family,"—to more complex ideas such as "when you help someone," or "doing things for other people to make them feel good."

Keep the Conversation Going by . . .
Asking when your child has felt love. What did it feel like? Why is love important? What would our family be like if we didn't all love each other? Where do you think love comes from? Do animals feel love?

DATE:_____ / _____ / _____

❏ *If you could be any age, what age do you think you would like the best?*

WHAT TO EXPECT

Each child will reflect on his or her life, where they have been and where they are going, as much as they are able to at their age. Expect most of your family members to want to be some age other than their current one. Most kids pick an older age because they think it means more freedom and less supervision. Children are always anxious to get to the next birthday and be bigger and older.

Keep the Conversation Going by . . .

Having your child tell you why she would want to be that age. What will be different in the future? Does she know anyone who is at that age now? If your child could live to be any age, how old would she want to be? 100? 120? What would be good about living so long? Be sure to share your own feelings about the perfect age.

DATE:_____ /_____ /_____

❑ *Would you rather have a fast car, a fast bicycle, or a fast boat?*

WHAT TO EXPECT

Anticipating and wanting are motivators, so this question will excite your children, particularly the younger ones. They will want the fast vehicle that best fits in with a fantasy. If your child has been wanting a new bike, that will be the answer. Many kids don't see themselves driving a boat or a car yet, so a bike is a safe answer that isn't scary. Older family members are likely to want the thing that they have the most use for and you can bet that teens will pick the car!

Keep the Conversation Going by . . .

Asking your child why she chose that particular option. What will that vehicle do that the others couldn't? What would she do with her vehicle? How fast will it go? Where will she go with it? Would she invite anyone along for the ride? What color would it be?

DATE:_____ /_____ /_____

❏ *If you could eat only three foods for a month, what three foods would you choose?*

WHAT TO EXPECT

This question should bring a smile to your children's faces. Expect them to think of forbidden fruits, so to speak. They are apt to put foods like chocolate ice cream, apple pie, and peanut butter cookies on their list. Pizza could also make an appearance, as well as whatever food your child is currently fixated on, like chicken nuggets or frosted cereal.

Keep the Conversation Going by . . .

Asking your child if he will get tired of eating just those foods. Why would he like to eat only those foods for a whole month? How does he think his body will feel if he eats just those foods? Are there foods that he will miss if he can only eat those three foods? Which foods are those? Why will he miss them? Offer your own list of three foods you could happily eat for a month.

TAKE A TIP:
WHEN AND HOW TO IGNORE

Inevitably, one of your kids will make a comment during the dinner conversation that is inappropriate. It might be mean-spirited, off-color, or too revealing. Being human, we all have a tendency to say things that we really shouldn't say. But once something is said, it can't be taken back. Now what?

Once an inappropriate remark has been made, there is no perfect response. But the worst thing you can do is to point out that the comment was inappropriate. Doing so does not restore the dignity of the child who was insulted or offended. After all, once a window is broken it cannot be fixed. Reprimanding the child who made the insult only keeps the spotlight on the person who was just insulted, adding injury to insult. Moreover, reprimanding the child who made the inappropriate remark tells that child that under some circumstances they are not emotionally safe at the dinner table. A person doesn't have to hear that very often before he or she will stop participating in the dinner conversations.

The best approach is to move on quickly. Make only a passing comment to acknowledge the person who spoke, and then direct a question to someone else. For example, you could say, "That's one way to answer that question." Then turning to another member of the family, you could quickly say, "Jason what do you think about . . . "

DATE:_____ /_____ /_____

❑ *Would you rather be a mountain climber, a scuba diver, or a spelunker?*

WHAT TO EXPECT

You might need to explain what a spelunker is if your children have never heard the term. This question will whet your children's appetite for adventure, so expect them to be talkative. They will most likely want to be the type of adventurer to which they have had the most exposure, but might jump on something that sounds new and exciting. The answers will help you further understand your child's interests.

Keep the Conversation Going by . . .

Asking your child what he knows about the three options. What does he know about spelunking? Mountain climbing? Scuba diving? Has he ever been in a store that had a lot of equipment used by mountain climbers or scuba divers? Has he ever seen any mountain climbers, scuba divers, or spelunkers in a movie or on television? Why would your child want to try the option he chose? Would he be scared to try it or just excited? How does he think he would feel right before he jumped, climbed, or entered the water?

DATE:_____ /_____ /_____

❑ *Clifford the Big Red Dog and the three-headed Fluffy from* Harry Potter and the Sorcerer's Stone *are two very different examples of giant dogs. If our family had a big dog, what would you want the dog to be like?*

WHAT TO EXPECT

Everyone has seen a large dog in real life, on television, or in a book. So no one will have trouble imagining the kind of dog they would like your family to have. Children six-years-old and younger will want a dog that will be a forgiving playmate. Of course, it might have unusual abilities, like the ability to talk, the ability to find lost things, or a knack for picking up messy rooms. Mom may want a dog that doesn't shed. Dad might want a hunting dog. This conversation could turn into a game where family members try to outdo each other in describing some very big dogs ("My dog is so big he…").

Keep the Conversation Going by . . .

Asking your child to tell you more about the dog. Where would such a dog sleep? How much would that dog eat in a day? What would the dog like to do? Play fetch? Sleep? Be patted? What would be the best thing about having a dog like this? Would there be any negatives? Has your child ever seen a dog that big? What would the dog's name be?

DATE: _____ / _____ / _____

❏ *Tell us about the most vivid or memorable dream you have ever had.*

WHAT TO EXPECT

Everyone has dreams, but dreams are rarely shared. Some children have recurring dreams and might describe such a dream. Others dream about things that happened to them during the previous day. Don't be surprised if you hear about some crazy dreams, since those are particularly memorable. If young children can't remember a dream and make up a story instead, that is okay.

Keep the Conversation Going by . . .

Having your child tell you when she had that dream. Has she ever had that dream or a dream like it before? Was the dream in color? Some people dream in color, but most people don't. How did your child feel when she woke up? Was she joyful? Scared? Angry? Anxious? Happy? What about the dream made her feel that way? Be sure to tell your child about your most vivid dream too.

DATE:_____ /_____ /_____

❑ *What is the neatest thing that you learned during the last week from someone in our family?*

WHAT TO EXPECT

Expect and permit a period of silence while everyone reflects on the last week. Eventually, someone will recall learning something from someone in the family, and the ideas will start to flow. This will likely evolve into a conversation where each family member shows appreciation for the way another one has contributed to his or her well-being and enhanced, even in a small way, his or her quality of life. However, sometimes people learn from the mistakes of others. So it is possible that your child will say something like, "I learned not to climb on the top of a step ladder when Dad fell and nearly broke his arm," or "I learned not to put bleach in with colored clothes when . . .".

Keep the Conversation Going by . . .

Having your child tell you how she learned that lesson. Did she watch something happen? Did someone tell her something new? When did that happen? What is the neatest thing your child has ever learned from someone in your family? Tell your child what you have learned this week from her.

DATE:_____ /_____ /_____

❑ *A long time ago, when a Lakota boy became a warrior, he put all the things that had personal meaning into a small pouch called a medicine bag. If you had a medicine bag, what small but meaningful things would you put in it?*

WHAT TO EXPECT

This question will cause your children to reflect on what is meaningful to them and how a small item can symbolize or represent that meaningful thing. Children will be the first to answer this question, as their well of significant things is not too deep. They may name items that they like to play with or which they think are interesting or fun, such as a toy car, unusual rock, or pretty barrette. The adults at the table will take longer, carefully searching through their memories for the most significant events and selecting those that provide a complete picture of their lives.

Keep the Conversation Going by . . .

Asking your child why she would put those particular things in her medicine bag. What do those things remind her of? Does she feel that those things offer protection as well? Would she show anyone what was inside her medicine bag or would she keep it to herself? Would her medicine bag be complete after she put those things into it, or would she want to keep adding to it as she got older?

DATE:_____ /_____ /_____

❏ *Every year, the Profile in Courage Award honors someone who has selflessly stuck by an unpopular decision or conviction in order to make other people's lives better or simply to do what was right. If you could give this award to someone you know, who would you give it to and why?*

WHAT TO EXPECT

This is a difficult question for children ten and under because they don't evaluate other people's behavior with a lot of depth. So you should give your answer to this question first. If feasible, pick someone that the family actually knows. That will make this idea more real and personal for your children and will suggest people that they might nominate for the award. You can also bend the rules and allow your children to look into the past to choose a nominee.

Keep the Conversation Going by . . .

Having your child tell you why he thinks that particular person did that selfless thing. When did he or she do that? How much courage does your child think it took to do that? What selfless thing has he done that he'd like to be awarded for? What other awards could your child give out to people? If he could give someone an award for being a fast runner, for example, whom would he give it to?

DATE:_____ /_____ /_____

❑ *If you had $50 to buy three new things, what would you buy?*

WHAT TO EXPECT

What people buy with their money tells a lot about their priorities and values. Your children will probably want to buy things that they will use for play or for their own use (like clothes or accessories) and adults will most often buy things that they need. Only an occasional person will think of buying things for someone else.

Keep the Conversation Going by . . .

Having your child tell you more about why he chose those items. What store would have them? Does he have anything like that already? If so, why does he need something so similar? How long does he think those items will last before he has to buy replacements? If he had an unlimited amount of money to spend, what three things would your child buy? If he had to buy three things and give them away, what would he buy and to whom would he give them?

DATE:_____ /_____ /_____

❑ *What outfit are you wearing when you feel you look your best?*

WHAT TO EXPECT

You will get some insight into how much thought your children have given to how they look, to what clothes they look best in, and to how clothes make them feel about themselves. Personality differences may surface with this question. Some children will be able to answer this question without much reflection and they will be very specific about an outfit. Some children are apt to shake their heads and have a hard time naming a specific outfit in their wardrobe.

Keep the Conversation Going by . . .

Asking your child about the last time she wore that outfit. Did anything special happen when she wore it? What about that outfit makes her feel good about herself? Have other people commented on how she looks in that outfit? How did she feel when she was complimented? What kinds of occasions or events warrant wearing that outfit? Does she wear it often?

DATE: _____ / _____ / _____

❑ *If you were to wear a wig, what color and style of wig would you pick out?*

WHAT TO EXPECT

Most people do not wear wigs, so expect this conversation starter to elicit giggles and even laughter. Girls may take this question seriously, and may think of a wig that compliments their looks or emulates an adored character, like Cinderella. Boys might suggest outlandish wigs that they would not, in their wildest dreams, actually wear, but which sound funny and crazy to them.

Keep the Conversation Going by . . .

Having your child tell you how he thinks you would act if he showed up to breakfast in that wig one day. Where would he want to go to show off his new look? How does he think others would react to him if he were wearing that wig? What would happen if his hair actually looked like that? How would he feel about that? Would he be excited or would he be embarrassed? Can he think of people who actually wear wigs (i.e. cancer patients, performers)?

DATE:_____ /_____ /_____

❑ *If someone wrote a song about you, what would that song be about? What might some of the words be?*

WHAT TO EXPECT

Each child will need to reflect about his or her prominent characteristics and qualities. Your children under the age of nine will think of light, hilarious, and even frivolous songs that talk about what they'd like to be known for. For example, songs like "He is the coolest dude in school." Older kids are apt to think about songs that tell what they'd like to become. The others at the dinner table are more likely to think of songs that capture their best qualities.

Keep the Conversation Going by . . .

Encouraging your child to tell you more about her song. Would that song become a hit? What would be the song's tune? What kind of song would it be? A happy song? A sad song? A dance song? Would people listen to the song years from now? Who does she know that might write a song like that about her? Would she like to have a song written about her? What is her favorite song? Why?

DATE: _____ / _____ / _____

❑ *If you played or worked outside all day long, what would you do to keep yourself from getting bored?*

WHAT TO EXPECT

In this day and age, many children rely on electronic devices from televisions to iPods to entertain them. It is good to at least think about how things would be different without them. Families who frequently experience the outdoors will have an easier time with this question by citing activities such as zoo trips, camping, swimming at a lake, skiing, or bicycling. You are apt to hear children offer play ideas which may not keep them occupied for more than thirty minutes. It is likely that the adults will be able to think of more time-consuming activities and work-related activities.

Keep the Conversation Going by . . .

Asking your child how long he thinks he'd like to do that thing. Why would he choose to do that activity? What is the longest amount of time he has played or worked outside by himself? Does he think that he is easily bored or does it take a long time for him to feel that way? Why does he think that is?

DATE:_____ /_____ /_____

❏ *If you were entering a talent contest, what would your talent be?*

WHAT TO EXPECT

This conversation starter will prompt your kids to think about their own exceptional talents. Expect younger children to claim talents they really don't have, but which might be things they wish they could do. Older children probably will talk about emerging talents. Adults are likely to mention areas of talent in which they once showed promise, but have long set aside. If that is the case, your children will enjoy hearing that Dad once played the drums.

Keep the Conversation Going by . . .

Asking your child to tell you more about her talent. When is the last time she practiced the talent? How does she think the judges would vote? Where does she think her talent came from? Was it passed down from a parent or relative? Does she know anyone else with that talent that she could perform with? Would she want to perform with anyone? How does she think she would feel right before she got on stage to perform? Scared? Excited? Nervous?

DATE: _____ / _____ / _____

❏ *What can playing a game tell you about your teammates and opponents?*

WHAT TO EXPECT

Games are an important part of socialization. This conversation starter will give you a sense of whether your child has age-appropriate socialization skills. Children six-years-old and younger do more parallel play than interactive play in games. When they do play team sports, the emphasis tends to be more on fun than on competition. Expect answers that have to do with sharing or being nice to each other. As they get older, children begin to play more competitive and team sports and have a better understanding about what makes a good team player and opponent. These children will talk about being a good loser, playing fair, and supporting the team.

Keep the Conversation Going by . . .

Asking your child who his favorite opponent is. Why does he like to play against that person? What game does he like to play? When did he last play that game? Does your child usually win or lose when he plays that game? Is there anyone he doesn't like to play against? Who does he like to have on his team for team games?

DATE:_____ /_____ /_____

❑ *Who has more fun, boys or girls?*

WHAT TO EXPECT

This conversation should elicit an animated exchange. Your children of each gender will enthusiastically argue their case. However, you will want to be alert for the child who thinks that the opposite gender has more fun. Anyone who expresses that sentiment might have low self-esteem that you'll want to address.

Keep the Conversation Going by . . .

Encouraging your child to tell you more about what he or she loves about being a boy or a girl. What are the differences? Has he or she thought very much about that? What are the similarities between boys and girls? What is good about both the similarities and the differences? Is there anything he or she can do to make life even more fun and exciting?

DATE:_____ /_____ /_____

☐ *What are the things, events, or people that have strongly influenced or impacted you?*

WHAT TO EXPECT

Most of us don't reflect a lot on the things that have influenced our lives. So expect a period of silence while everyone ponders the question. Your children will probably talk about friends, family members, pets, and exciting family events (such as big trips or holidays) that have left a big impression on them, or which they are currently excited about. You can expect the adolescents in the family to name a teacher, as good teachers coming along at the right time often have a strong influence on young people. As an adult you can talk about the things that have deeply impacted you. Listening to this will help your children gain some perspective and come to understand you better.

Keep the Conversation Going by . . .

Having your child tell you more about that event or person. Was she positively or negatively influenced? Did she know at the time that that person or event was going to strongly influence her? How would her life be different if that person or event had not come along or happened? Does she think that she has had a strong influence on someone else? Who?

DATE:_____ /_____ /_____

❏ *Would you like to live in another country?*

WHAT TO EXPECT

Children tend to think that where they live is the only place to live. The adults at the table should start the conversation and point out things like language differences, differences in freedom, standard of living, and so on. This will help your children visualize the differences and then offer their opinions about them. They might comment on how hard it would be to live someplace where they couldn't understand what people were saying or how they wouldn't like living in a hut.

Keep the Conversation Going by . . .

Asking your child why he would want to live in another country. What would the benefits be? Better food? Exotic locales? Would there be any disadvantages? Missing family? Has there ever been a time when he thought about traveling to another country to work, learn, or live? Does he know anyone who has moved to another country or has lived in another country in the past?

DATE:_____ /_____ /_____

❑ *What would it be like if you woke up one morning and there wasn't any gravity?*

WHAT TO EXPECT

Imagining things being different than they seem has led scientists to great insights and it is a good mental exercise for all of us, especially children, to think "what if?" Your children will probably initially react with ideas about how fun it would be to float around like they've seen astronauts do. As the family discusses the idea though, the real implications will begin to sink in for them and they will talk about chairs floating around and difficulty using the bathroom.

Keep the Conversation Going by . . .

Asking your child to think about some specific situations which the lack of gravity might affect. Where would he have to hold a glass when he pours himself a glass of milk? Would his hat still stay on his head? What would a leaf do when it falls off a tree? Would he float out of bed at night? Would it be hard to get anywhere if everything else was floating around in the air too? Would your home stay in one place? Would he float away into outer space?

DATE:_____ /_____ /_____

❑ *How would you finish the sentence "Someday I will . . . ?"*

WHAT TO EXPECT

This question should prompt everyone at the dinner table to think about the things that they would like to do in the future and it should help your children understand that someday seldom happens unless they do something to make it happen. Expect everyone at the dinner table to have something to say. The only difference will be the time frame. Younger children are apt to have a shorter time frame for their "someday" than the older members of your family, so expect your kids to focus on things they are looking forward to, such as buying a cell phone, getting a gerbil, playing on a football team, or other things that are related to current interests. Be sure to add your own "someday" dreams as well.

Keep the Conversation Going by . . .

Asking your child how long she has wanted this thing to happen. Is it something she just thought of or has she been thinking about it for a while? When does she think this "someday" will happen? Is there anything she can or will do to help make this happen?

DATE:_____ /_____ /_____

❑ *What kind of car would you design for us to use in the future?*

WHAT TO EXPECT

This question will strengthen children's awareness of the world and its energy issues. It is also intended to encourage them to think creatively about designing a product. Children love to think about cars and how to make them go. So the adults at the table might be surprised at some of the interesting and unique car designs that their children develop. Encourage your child to think about what would power the car and expect interesting answers like milk, dirt, air, and cereal.

Keep the Conversation Going by . . .

Encouraging your child to give more details about her car. How fast would her car go? What would her car look like? What safety features would her car have? Would it look like the cars she sees now or would it be completely different from anything anyone has ever seen before? How would be it be better than cars that use gas?

DATE:_____ /_____ /_____

❑ *If our family were to start a business,*
   what kind of business would it be?

WHAT TO EXPECT

This is another question that will prompt your children
to see the relationship between what they do today and
what is going to happen tomorrow. Everyone at the table
should be able to contribute equally well to this conversation. Children will initially choose a business that
appeals to them, like a candy store, motorcycle store,
or pet store. As the conversation moves along, they will
notice others focusing on the family's skills and talents
and may be able to focus in on what your family would
actually be good at doing, such as repairing computers
or selling antiques.

Keep the Conversation Going by . . .

Having your child tell you more about her ideas for
the family business. What would her role be? What will
other people like about the business? How would your
child promote the family business? How would she get
people to notice what your family is doing? Would she
advertise with an ad in the paper? A bake sale? Something completely different? Where will the business be
located? Would she like to run that business someday?
What would be the perks of running her own business?
The disadvantages?

196

DATE:_____ /_____ /_____

❑ *What do you think about before you fall asleep?*

WHAT TO EXPECT
There is something to the saying that there are two kinds of people in the world: optimists and pessimists. If your children are optimists, expect them to be thinking of all the neat things that tomorrow is going to bring or all the neat things that happened today. If your children are pessimists, they may worry about what tomorrow might bring or ruminate about things that did not go so well today. Everyone at the dinner table will be able to share his or her thoughts on this one. However, some children will say that they go to bed without thinking about anything but brushing their teeth, putting on their pajamas, and crawling into bed. Maybe they are the realists.

Keep the Conversation Going by . . .
Asking your child why he thinks about the things that he thinks about at night. Do they help him fall asleep or do they keep him awake? How does he help himself fall asleep if he's having trouble? Does he count sheep? Do multiplication tables? How does he feel when he thinks about these things? Does he ever have dreams that connect to things he thinks about before falling asleep? What happens in those dreams?

DATE:_____ /_____ /_____

❑ *What would be the best part about being four years old again?*

WHAT TO EXPECT

It may be hard for your children to exactly remember what happened when they were four—all those preschool years may seem to blend together. Older family members will reflect back, but you can expect your children to take this conversation starter as an opportunity to relive fun things. For example, one of them might say, "Remember the Christmas when I got a bicycle? I'd like to relive that Christmas." Those at the table who have lived long enough to make a few mistakes or to let a few good opportunities pass are apt to tell how they would like to make a few different decisions since that time.

Keep the Conversation Going by . . .

Asking your child if she would want to relive things just as they happened, or if she want a few things to happen differently. If she would like to change some things, what would she change and why? What does she know now that she wishes she had known then? What are some good things about not being four years old anymore? More freedom? Going to school? More friends? What differences does your child see between children who are four years old and children who are older?

DATE:_____ /_____ /_____

❑ *If you could turn your bedroom into a theme room that focused on only one thing, what would you make it look like?*

WHAT TO EXPECT

Your children will enjoy letting their imaginations run free and considering the themes they might want to have. The younger the child, the more unique they will think about making their bedroom decor. A four-year-old boy might want his bedroom to look like the inside of an Indian teepee. A six-year-old girl might want her bedroom to look like a park. Older children might stick with things they are very involved with, like baseball or dance.

Keep the Conversation Going by . . .

Having your child tell you about the inspiration behind her room redesign. Why would she pick that theme for her room? Would she really like to make those changes or is this idea just a passing thought? If she would really like that, what are some things she could do to make it look like that? Would it be realistic to make those changes or would they just be fun to see?

DATE:_____ / _____ / _____

❑ *Tell us your favorite story about your grandparents.*

WHAT TO EXPECT

Your children will likely recall fun times they spent with grandparents, such as going to a fair or going to the zoo. Depending on the personality of the grandparents, you might hear funny stories about silly things the grandparents did to make your kids laugh. Adults are apt to reflect back on their own grandparents' best qualities and may tell stories that discuss experiences that hardened their grandparents or established their core values. This also gives you an opportunity to tell a story about the children's grandparents that the children had not before heard. Such stories strengthen family bonds and give children a sense of connectedness.

Keep the Conversation Going by . . .

Asking your child to tell you why she chose to tell that particular story. How does she think that experience affected her grandparents? Did it make them stronger? Does she think they enjoyed that experience? Did that experience bring her grandparents closer to their grandchildren?

DATE:_____ /_____ /_____

❑ *What is worth fighting for?*

WHAT TO EXPECT

The conversation will vary considerably in nature depending on the ages of the children at the table. Your children who are younger than seven will likely consider playground scuffles and arguments with siblings. Older children may see the question in a broader sense and might say it is worth fighting for something when you're right or to protect someone.

Keep the Conversation Going by . . .

Asking your child if he has ever been in a fight. If so, was it a physical or verbal fight? Who was the fight with? What was the fight over? Was this worth fighting for? What was the outcome? How did he feel after the fight had ended? Did anyone know about this fight before now? Would he fight about the same thing again?

DATE:_____ /_____ /_____

❏ *If you could encounter any mythical or imaginary creature, such as the Loch Ness monster, a unicorn, or Big Foot, which one would you pick?*

WHAT TO EXPECT

Expect your children to focus on a creature that they have recently read or heard about and which is of immediate interest to them. If you just watched a TV show about Nessie, that could be the answer. If a book about Big Foot came home from the library, that will likely affect the response. This question will give your children the opportunity to fantasize and imagine different scenarios without fear.

Keep the Conversation Going by . . .

Asking why your child chose that creature. Would the creature be friendly? Would your child invite it home? Would she be afraid of it? What stories might the creature have to tell? Would your child tell anyone else about the creature or keep it a secret? How might other people react?

DATE:_____ /_____ /_____

❑ *Was there ever a specific time when you thought you were going to die?*

WHAT TO EXPECT

Most older people have had life-threatening experiences, usually involving car accidents or near accidents. And anyone who has ever been in an airplane as it flew through moderate turbulence has had at least fleeting thoughts that the end might be near. Those thoughts of death had at least some basis in reality. However, younger children sometimes think that they might die soon even though there is no objective basis for their fear. You will want to listen carefully to what your youngest children say. It might be necessary to clarify some misconceptions or to give assurances. Don't be surprised if your child thought he was going to die in a situation that does not strike you as serious—such as being embarrassed by a teacher or crossing a street. There are some children who have never had this feeling, so be open to that response.

Keep the Conversation Going by . . .

Asking your child to tell you about the last time she thought she might die. Why did she feel this way? What situation was she in? What did she do? Looking back, does it seem as though she could really have died?

DATE: _____ / _____ / _____

❑ *Finish the sentence "I occasionally have a crazy idea to...."*

WHAT TO EXPECT

Expect your children to share inner thoughts that they often have but don't share because they think someone will laugh at them or disregard them. Your children will likely make up a spur-of-the-moment, attention-getting, crazy idea. If they do, enjoy the idea with them. Older people at the table might share something they have been giving serious thought to but never talked about for fear that it would be disregarded or mocked.

Keep the Conversation Going by . . .

Having your child tell you what it would take for him to act on that crazy idea. Does he think that he might just do it someday? Would acting on that idea be danger-ous? What precautions, if any, could he take to make it safer? Why is this idea something your child would like to do? What about the idea seems interesting to him?

DATE:_____ /_____ /_____

❑ *If something was broken and you had to
fix it but didn't know how, what would
you do?*

WHAT TO EXPECT

The responses to this conversation starter will vary
depending upon each person's experience at fixing
things that are broken. Your children will likely first say
they would try to fix it themselves with glue or tape.
When you point out that the question is what would
he do if he didn't know how to fix it but needed to,
they will think about how they might find out. They may
say they would ask you. Children who have had some
experience using the Internet may suggest looking for
an answer there. This conversation starter helps your
children think through how to solve a problem. You
can share how you learned how to fix something and
where you got the information.

Keep the Conversation Going by . . .

Asking your child if she has ever tried to fix something that was broken. What did she try to fix? Was she
the one who broke it? Was she successful at fixing this
item? Has she ever become really frustrated when trying to fix something? How did she deal with that frustration? How good is her track record at fixing things?

DATE: _____ / _____ / _____

❑ *Who in this world do you think is in the most need of help?*

WHAT TO EXPECT

This question will prompt your children to think about others, especially people in need of food, shelter, water, and medical care. Everyone at the table will know of someone or some group of people in this world in need of help. The kind of help mentioned may depend on your family's culture, religion, or values, as well as what they've recently seen or heard about at school or on TV. In some families, children may talk about people who need help learning about Jesus. In other families, children may talk about people who need help after a natural disaster. In yet other families, children may mention people in town who don't have enough to eat.

Keep the Conversation Going by . . .

Encouraging your child to think of ways that he can help. What can he do to make things better for those people? What kind of help do these people need? Whose responsibility is it to help those people? What could your family do together to provide help?

DATE:_____ /_____ /_____

❑ *What is the craziest outfit you have ever worn?*

WHAT TO EXPECT

Your children will laugh at themselves and with each other as they recall a particularly crazy outfit they have worn, often at Halloween or when playing dress up. Expect your children to make something up or at least wildly exaggerate an outfit. Children over age eight may talk about an outfit their mother or father made them wear when they were younger and which they thought (maybe even knew) was hideous. Children might also remind you of photos that show them in outfits they did not like. The adults at the dinner table will reflect back to outfits that were once very much in fashion, but now are recognized for the awful things they were.

Keep the Conversation Going by . . .

Asking your child why she wore that crazy outfit. Just for fun? For Halloween? Would she ever wear something like that again? Who saw her wearing that crazy outfit? What does she think people thought when they saw her outfit? Did anyone say anything to her about how she looked? What is the craziest outfit she has ever seen someone else wear? Who wore it and where?

DATE:_____ /_____ /_____

❏ *Would you rather be a veterinarian, a dentist, or a pediatrician?*

WHAT TO EXPECT

This question will help expand the vocabulary of young children who might not have thought about different names for different types of doctors. Once the terms are defined, children could participate at all levels considering what they would like or dislike about each profession. Your child has probably pretended to be a doctor at some point and this will allow him to describe that fantasy. Kids who are into animals are likely to choose the veterinarian. Children who have particular fears about dentists or shots at the pediatrician will shy away from those choices.

Keep the Conversation Going by . . .

Asking your child how someone might decide to become a special kind of doctor. What qualities do people need to have if they are going to spend their lives taking care of others? Does your child feel that she has those qualities? How do people decide what they want to be when they grow up? What does she want to be when she grows up? Has she considered being a special doctor?

DATE: _____ / _____ / _____

❑ *When you see people on the street asking for money, what thoughts go through your head?*

WHAT TO EXPECT

This question is designed to encourage your children to think about societal issues and their social responsibility with respect to these problems. Children younger than eight are likely to take the situation at face value and assume the person needs help. Older children are apt to be particularly sensitive to the plight of such people because they can imagine what it might be like to be homeless or hungry. Adolescents are probably worldly enough to know that some people who ask for money may use it to buy drugs or alcohol.

Keep the Conversation Going by . . .

Asking your child why he thinks those people are asking for money. What does he think they need to buy? How does being asked for money make him feel? What would determine whether he gives any of them money? Does he think there are people in your town who sometimes ask others for money? Who would he ask if he needed money? How else could people like this get help?

DATE:_____ /_____ /_____

❑ *What would be the best thing about having a bigger family?*

WHAT TO EXPECT

Your children likely see their family composition as static. It is the way it is, and it could not be otherwise. It is useful for them to consider alternatives. Some children at the table might think a bigger family would be a good thing. They could envision having more brothers or sisters to play with. Other children will not like the idea. They will be fearful that the same resources, both material and immaterial, will need to be spread further, meaning they will get less of both.

Keep the Conversation Going by . . .

Asking your child if she would want a bigger family. Is she happy with the way things are now? How much bigger could the family be? How much bigger would she like the family to be? If she could choose, would she want to be the youngest member in this expanded family or the oldest? Would she want a brother or a sister, or one—or more—of each? Does she know anyone who has a large family? How large? What does she think about it?

DATE: _____ / _____ / _____

❑ *Many people collect things—stamps, matchbook covers, coins, dolls, farm tractors, old cars, cookbooks, etc. What would you like to collect?*

WHAT TO EXPECT

It is human nature to want more of something that interests us. If your children have collections, you won't be surprised by their answers. However, some children may shock you by announcing they collect things you had no idea they were interested in–bottle caps, stickers, pigs, or rocks. This conversation can open your eyes to interests you weren't even aware of. You can share information about your own collections and help your children understand the value of collections.

Keep the Conversation Going by . . .

Asking your child if he has already started his collection. How would he go about increasing his collection? Where could he get more items? Does it take a lot of money to buy the things that he'd like to collect? Once he was finished collecting that item, if he stretched his collection out in a line, how far does he think that line would reach? Across the lawn? Down the street? Across the street? Around the world? To the moon?

DATE:_____ / _____ / _____

❑ *Describe your idea of a perfect day. What would you do, where would you go, and who would you share your perfect day with?*

WHAT TO EXPECT

This conversation starter will prompt your children to think about what kind of day would be enjoyable and fun. It should also prompt them to ask themselves what they might be able to do to help someone when they seem to need a special day. Your children may describe days that are actually attainable or fantasy days such as when a seven-year-old boy says his perfect day would be spent as an astronaut on a space ship.

Keep the Conversation Going by . . .

Having your child tell you if she has ever done any of those things that would make a day perfect. Does she think that she might have such a perfect day, or at least something close to it in the future?

DATE:_____ /_____ /_____

❑ *What is the most important thing that adults should remember?*

WHAT TO EXPECT
Both you and your children will get an opportunity to hear what is important to the other. Your children are likely to comment on your behavior as it impacts them and could say things like, "You should remember not to get mad," or, "They should remember to play with me." Adults at the table are apt to think about family responsibilities that are important.

Keep the Conversation Going by . . .
Having your child tell you how often he thinks adults think about this important thing. Does he think adults think about this at all? Why is it important for adults to keep this in mind? Is this something that is important for all adults to remember or just the adults in our family? What other things should adults remember to think about? Put the shoe on the other foot and take the time to tell your child what you think kids should remember. Is this something your child has thought of before?

DATE: _____ / _____ / _____

❑ *If you could choose anyone other than us to be your parents, who would you choose?*

WHAT TO EXPECT

You can be sure your kids have fantasized about this one before, so they will be quick to give you some answers. Celebrities, friends' parents, beloved teachers, or grandparents are likely to come up in the discussion. Kids will focus in on adults with whom they have positive associations. This is a chance for them to enjoy sticking it to you a little bit as they imagine what great parents all of these people would make.

Keep the Conversation Going by . . .

Asking your child why she chose those substitute parents. What would those parents do differently? What kinds of rules would they have? Would they know how to take care of her? What kinds of things would they do with her?

DATE:_____/_____/_____

❑ *If you were to start a band, what would be your role in the band and what would you call the band?*

WHAT TO EXPECT

All children younger than twelve are convinced that they have musical talent. So their musical talent or lack thereof will not constrain their aspirations. Instead, the role they want to play in their band will depend more upon the musician they idolize. Guitar, drums, and vocals are apt to be the popular picks by your children. They will come up with band names that mimic names of bands they like, but as the discussion goes on some names might come up that are a little crazy and silly.

Keep the Conversation Going by . . .

Asking your child what kind of music his band will play. How many people will be in the band? What instruments need to be in the band? Where would he go on tour? What would he title his CD? How would he dress for concerts? Who would he thank in his Grammy acceptance speech?

DATE:_____/_____/_____

❑ *There is a story that George Washington once said, "I cannot tell a lie." What would life be like if no one could lie?*

WHAT TO EXPECT

Your children will think about the kinds of lies they might tell and realize that if they couldn't lie, they could not hide things they did wrong. You've already taught them it is wrong to lie, but they will recognize that they do lie on occasion. They may not want to admit many of their past lies to you since they are certain you don't know about them! Don't press them to reveal lies, but get them to think about a future without lies.

Keep the Conversation Going by . . .

Asking your child to tell you why she thinks people lie. How can lies hurt people? Does she think white lies are a good thing or a bad thing? Would it be hard for her to tell the truth all the time for an entire week? Are there some people that like to tell a lot of lies? Why does she think they do that?

DATE:_____ /_____ /_____

❑ *What do you think would be the hardest part about being a rock star?*

WHAT TO EXPECT

We tend to view many jobs from a distance and see only the glamorous parts of them. This question might help your children realize that there are downsides to even the most desirable of jobs. The children at the table will initially have trouble identifying any aspect of being a rock star that is difficult because their immediate impression is all about the glamour and fun involved. You can help them to think about the hard part of the job by pointing out a few downsides, such as traveling all the time, having to practice a lot, and convincing people to buy your music. Once you get your kids to think about the actual lifestyle and responsibilities involved, they will come up with more downsides on their own. Indeed, one of them might mention something like, "I think it would be hard work being the drummer. They are always going ninety miles an hour."

Keep the Conversation Going by . . .

Asking your child to put herself in a rock star's shoes. How often does she think they get to see their family? What would it be like to travel from place to place in a bus? After you've discussed the disadvantages of being a rock star, have fun talking about the advantages that rock stars likely enjoy.

DATE:_____ /_____ /_____

❑ *What is the most unusual thing you've
ever seen happen at a birthday party?*

WHAT TO EXPECT

Children love birthday parties; and by the time they are
ten or eleven, most of them have gone to a lot of them.
They will jump right on this conversation starter and
share stories about cake being thrown, balloons being
popped, and clowns putting on shows. They may recall
unusual gifts, birthday children who cried, or guests
who misbehaved. The stories that are shared are certain to be very entertaining to everyone at the table.
Share some of your memories about unusual birthday
happenings as well.

Keep the Conversation Going by . . .

Having your child tell you more about what went on
at the party. When did that unusual thing happen? How
did it happen? Who was at that particular party? Did
anyone else see this unusual thing happen? If so, how
did they react? Did the adults react differently than the
other kids? If so, how? Be sure to remind your child of
something unusual that happened at one of her own
birthday parties.

DATE:_____ /_____ /_____

❏ *Finish this sentence5: "I have…"*

WHAT TO EXPECT

With such an open-ended conversation starter it is impossible to predict how your children will respond—and that is what makes it so interesting! So expect this conversation starter to elicit a few surprise comments. Your child could say, "I have a booger in my nose," "I have to go to the bathroom," "I have a stuffed turtle," or "I have math homework." If you want to use this as a way to make a big announcement, Dad might say, "I have a new job." Mom might say, "I have an important announcement. We will soon have an addition to our family."

Keep the Conversation Going by . . .

Asking your child how long he has had that. How does he feel about it? You can even make this conversation starter into a game. Go around the table and have each person say what they have. Try to keep the items in alphabetical order. For example, the first person could say, "I have an A+ in my class." The second could say, "I have a banana." And so on.

DATE:_____ /_____ /_____

❏ *Talk about a time when you had to for-give someone and give him or her a sec-ond chance.*

WHAT TO EXPECT

Being offended or wronged by someone and then for-giving is a skill we practice more as adolescents and especially as adults since we often have no choice but to do our best to preserve relationships and workplace associations. So the adults and older children at the table should be the first to address this conversation starter. They can model its meaning for the younger children. Children are sensitive to offenses, however, they typically forget them quickly and move past them. Your child will likely focus on something a friend or sibling did. "Jonathan broke my robot. But I played with him again the next day." He may not have really thought at the time about the fact that this meant he forgave his friend, so this conversation can help him identify that in retrospect.

Keep the Conversation Going by . . .

Asking your child to tell you more about the situation. When did that happen? Does your child think that per-son did it on purpose? How long did it take him to for-give and offer his friend a second chance? Was it hard for him to forgive his friend? Did forgiving and offering that second chance prove to be a good idea? Has any-one ever had to forgive him for something he's done?

DATE:_____ /_____ /_____

❑ *Whom do you allow to tell you what to do?*

WHAT TO EXPECT

When plotted by age, there is a U-shaped response curve with regard to number of people individuals let tell them what to do. Expect children under the age of ten and family members over the age of twenty to identify numbers of people who occasionally tell them what to do: parents, teachers, bosses, an occasional friend or co-worker, spouses. Family members between these two ages are apt to think that no one ever tells them what to do. This conversation will allow children to reflect on who influences them and might help them gain insight into understanding the people who have influence on them.

Keep the Conversation Going by . . .

Asking your child how she feels when a person tells her what to do. Does she like it when certain people tell her what to do? Does it make her angry? Does it depend on what the person is telling her or who the person is? Does she generally do what this person tells her to do? Is there anyone that she wishes she could tell what to do? If so, what kinds of things would she tell that person?

DATE:_____ /_____ /_____

❑ *What song best reflects your thoughts and personality?*

WHAT TO EXPECT

Each of your children will be able to share a song that he or she enjoys. Expect them to select a song that is currently popular, or a standard that is well-known in your family. If your child sees herself as peppy and fun, she might pick a dance tune. Children who are interested in being cool or tough might pick a rap or hip hop song. Be sure to share a song that you think embodies your personality and feel free to pick something silly to get a few laughs, such as a song by the Chipmunks or a current song that is clearly not you.

Keep the Conversation Going by . . .

Encouraging your child to tell you why she connects to that particular song. Where was she when she first heard that song? What are some of the words? Have her sing a little of it. Have her explain the connection between the song lyrics and her thoughts and personality. How long has it been since she last heard that song? Does she connect to other songs when she is in different moods?

DATE: _____ / _____ / _____

❑ *Tell about a time when you did some-thing to surprise someone. What was their reaction?*

WHAT TO EXPECT

You will gain insight into how much time, effort, and consideration your child put into surprising this person. Planning surprises can be a creative outlet for some people. People with a strong sense of humor also tend to enjoy surprising others. There will be a correlation of age and how much time the person spent planning the surprise. Children might respond with stories of making a card or gift for you, keeping a secret about their birthday present for a friend, or jumping out from behind a door to scare a sibling.

Keep the Conversation Going by . . .

Having your child tell you about how he planned this surprise. Did he have help? Did this surprise work the way he had hoped? Was there anything he would have liked to have done, but wasn't able to do? Looking back on it, would he plan a surprise like this again? If he could plan a surprise with unlimited resources (time, money, space, etc.) what would that surprise be like and who would he choose to surprise?

DATE:_____ /_____ /_____

❑ *You're at a very fancy restaurant. You take a bite of your food and it is truly horrible tasting. What do you do?*

WHAT TO EXPECT

Your children under the age of seven will blurt out their immediate reaction, which would be to just spit it out. The older your child, the more likely he is to think about social conventions and might consider using a napkin to spit it out, running to the bathroom to spit it out, or even (for your bravest children) swallowing it. Don't criticize your children's honest answers. Instead, work through all the alternatives and how and when each one might be appropriate.

Keep the Conversation Going by . . .

Finding out about the most horrible thing your child ever tasted and how he reacted. Why does he think adults refrain from spitting out food they don't like? What are some other things he thinks might not be appropriate to do at the dinner table? Which ones has he done? Who has taught him the table manners he has? Does he think they are hard rules to follow?

DATE:_____ /_____ /_____

❑ *Tell us your favorite holiday and a memory of something special that happened on that holiday.*

WHAT TO EXPECT

Sharing positive, family-based memories strengthens family ties. You can expect Christmas, Hanukkah, or other holidays your family celebrates that focus on children in a positive way to be the favorite holiday of your children younger than eleven because it is the holiday when they get a lot of things or do fun things. They'll talk about gifts they got, special food, and surprises that happened to them. For some adults, the favorite holiday could be a more religious day like Easter or a day centered on family togetherness like Thanksgiving.

Keep the Conversation Going by . . .

Having your child tell you more about his favorite holiday. Why is that his favorite holiday? What makes that holiday special? Would it be as fun if gifts were not involved? What traditions does your family repeat year after year that he loves? What year was that special memory made? Who was there? Does he think the other people there also have a special memory from that day? Tell your child if you remember that day and also share your favorite holiday memories with those at the table.

DATE:_____ /_____ /_____

❑ *Tell us about a time you got lost.*

WHAT TO EXPECT

At one time or another, everyone has gotten lost. Even the youngest child in the family is apt to have a distinct memory of being lost, even if it was being temporarily separated from a parent in the mall. It is useful for children to learn that their parents also make mistakes and therefore are human. It is also useful for children to hear about problem-solving strategies for when they do get lost.

Keep the Conversation Going by . . .

Asking your child to tell you how she felt when she was lost. Was she scared? Surprised? Anxious? How did she find out where she needed to go? Did she ask someone to help her? Did she figure it out on her own? Did you or someone else find her without her having to do anything? Can she think of a time when it might be fun to be lost? Maybe in a corn maze or when exploring a new area with you?

DATE:_____ /_____ /_____

❏ *Who knows you best?*

WHAT TO EXPECT

This conversation starter will help you see who your child feels most closely aligned with. Answers could include you, a grandparent, a friend, or a sibling. Children are apt to pick someone they spend a lot of conflict-free time with. Be sure to share your answer as well so your child can begin to understand adult friendships and relationships.

Keep the Conversation Going by . . .

Asking your child why she feels that this person knows her better than anyone else. Do they talk all the time? Do they play or hang out together? Is this person her best friend? Does she feel that she knows this person better than anyone else as well? Tell your child about the person you feel knew you best when you were growing up.

DATE:_____ /_____ /_____

❑ *Make up a sound that a giraffe might make. What would the giraffe be trying to communicate when it made that sound?*

WHAT TO EXPECT

Your children will make up some interesting sounds! They are likely to start with sounds that mimic other animals, but will then get more creative. They will try to top each other with their unusual sounds. Your children may come up with different sounds the giraffes use to convey different feelings, and this will show their awareness of different emotions.

Keep the Conversation Going by . . .

Asking your child if he has heard a giraffe make a sound, perhaps at a zoo or on a nature program on television. How can he find out what sounds a giraffe really makes? How do giraffes understand what each other are saying? How do baby giraffes learn to make noises? Does your child think there are any animals that don't make sounds? How do these animals communicate?

DATE:_____/_____/_____

❑ *What would happen if the whole world stopped using clocks to schedule when things started? For example, school would not start at 8:30. It would start when all of the students and the teacher got there.*

WHAT TO EXPECT

Your children will consider how this man-made concept has come to strongly impact nearly everyone in the world, in some cultures more than others. It will be interesting to start this conversation by asking the youngest member of the family first. He will like the idea of the world waiting for him at first ("I could wake up whenever I wanted to"), but as the conversation moves along, will come to realize some of the disadvantages of this idea ("We wouldn't know what time movies started").

Keep the Conversation Going by . . .

Encouraging your child to think about all the different effects of not using clocks. Can he see any advantages to not scheduling things by time? Have him list some advantages. He wouldn't have to rush? He could play with his friends for as long as he wanted? Would not using clocks create some problems? What problems can he think of? He would do a lot of waiting around? He wouldn't know when his favorite shows were on?

DATE:_____ /_____ /_____

❏ *What video game would you like to be in?*

WHAT TO EXPECT

Parents will learn a little about the electronic video world that daily impacts their children. The resulting discussion will help you bridge the gap that lies between you and your children. Your children will likely have an instant favorite to name with lots of good reasons for the choice. You'll learn more about video games than you ever imagined.

Keep the Conversation Going by . . .

Asking your child to tell you more about his favorite video game. What does he like the most about that game? Have him tell you about the goal of the game and what the graphics look like. What would he look like if he were in the game? Would he want to look like himself, like a character who is already in the game, or like something completely different? If he could create his own video game, what would that game be like?

DATE:_____ /_____ /_____

❑ *Finish this sentence: "I wonder what my life would be like if . . . "*

WHAT TO EXPECT

This conversation starter will give each of your children the opportunity to share his or her innermost thoughts. Expect your children to dream of what might be (they may come up with some very fanciful situations, such as "If I was made of marshmallow" or "If I had wheels instead of feet") and adults to reflect on what might have been. The answers will enlighten you as to what your children are dreaming of and what the adults at the table may feel they've missed.

Keep the Conversation Going by . . .

Asking your child to tell you why she wished or wishes that event had happened or will happen. How would that change her life? Have her tell you in detail what would be different. What would be the same? Does she think this might ever happen?

DATE:_____ /_____ /_____

❑ *What is the most important thing you would want your children to know about you?*

WHAT TO EXPECT

Each family member will reflect on the legacy that they are laying down within the family's historical lineage. Older family members will find this a sobering question to contemplate. Children will give more seemingly frivolous answers and may not have really thought about themselves being parents one day. They will likely focus in on what is important about them right now—such as, "I like ballet" or "I won a basketball trophy."

Keep the Conversation Going by . . .

Asking your child to tell you how he will ensure that his children know this important thing about him. Will they know this important thing from what they observe him doing or from what they hear him say about himself? Has your child ever thought about having children one day before you asked him this question? Make sure you tell your child what you want him to know about you and why.

DATE:_____ /_____ /_____

❏ *If our family were asked to make one room in a haunted house this coming Halloween, how would we make that room really scary?*

WHAT TO EXPECT

Everyone will have to do some creative thinking to come up with ideas for making the room scary. Your children will have a wealth of ideas for this question, but some of them might not be grounded in reality. Sit back and enjoy the descriptions of flying vampires, machines that change people into monsters, and disappearing floors.

Keep the Conversation Going by . . .

Having your child tell you more about her thoughts on what is scary. Will she put anything in the room that others may not be frightened of like bees or dogs? Does she have to worry about making the room too scary? What color will the room be? What will the outside of the haunted house look like? Who does your child see coming to her haunted house? Kids? Parents? Teens? Is the haunted house safe for everyone? Has she designed anything that could hurt someone?

DATE: _____ / _____ / _____

❏ *Finish this sentence "I love it when . . . "*

WHAT TO EXPECT

Your children will learn what makes another family member's day and are apt to mention actions or outcomes. For example, a six-year-old might say "I love it when you make chocolate chip cookies for my lunch." A ten-year-old might say, "I love it when I win at Guitar Hero." Answers will focus around your child's current passions.

Keep the Conversation Going by . . .

Encouraging your child to tell you about the last time this thing happened. Was anyone else involved? Is this thing more enjoyable when your child shares it with someone or does he like to enjoy it by himself?

DATE:_____ /_____ /_____

❏ *How would you build a house so that it used less fuel to heat it?*

WHAT TO EXPECT

Going green is becoming popular and, in many people's minds, critical. It is useful for children—and for adults as well—to think about what little things we can do to use less of the earth's resources. But this is a tough question. Expect to ask some leading questions to get your young children to think about how your home and family can use less of the earth's resources.

Keep the Conversation Going by . . .

Having your child think about different ways to get warm. For example, does standing in the sun or standing in the shade make her warmer? Does this give her an idea about one way for your house to use less fuel? Maybe the house should use the sun for heat? What temperature does your child think the thermostat should be set to in the winter? Could she save the planet by turning that down by just one degree? Why?

TAKE A TIP:
DEALING WITH WHOPPERS

Young children often make up stories and tell them so convincingly that you might be concerned that they believe them. For example, when talking about the most disgusting thing he's ever eaten, a preschooler might say, "I ate a worm one time. I put ketchup on it and then I ate it. But it tasted awful."

Children tell whoppers because they want to have something to say and, like all of us, they want their story to top everyone else's. However, some children tell whoppers which all have a common theme: I am fantastic. In these whoppers, the child is incredibly strong, amazingly brave, uncommonly smart, or unusually nice. Such whoppers indicate that the child has a low self-concept. If he can't be these things in real life, he will fantasize about having these qualities.

If your child tells a whopper, don't refute it. Pointing out that the story could not possibly be true robs the child of his dignity. Let the story stand unchallenged, but don't play into it. Just say, "That is an interesting story," then move the conversation in a different direction. Don't forget the underlying message that your child is conveying. Make a point to praise your child for the positive things he does. As you fill your child's void with encouragement, the telling of tall tales will gradually fade away.

DATE:_____ /_____ /_____

❑ *What would it be like to be a little person?*

WHAT TO EXPECT

Some children may not have heard this term before and will need to be told it refers to dwarfism. Once everyone is on board with the definition, your children will start to think through the implications. What will be interesting is that children under seven already have the experience of being small in a big world, so they will likely reflect on things they can't do, such as reach the kitchen faucet or the top shelf in their closets. Older children will come up with thoughts about driving cars, buying clothes, and managing in stores.

Keep the Conversation Going by . . .

Having your child consider what it might feel like to be an adult who is the size of a child. What kinds of changes would need to be made to a normal home for a little person? Where would she shop? Would people stare at her? How hard would it be to be so different?

DATE:_____ /_____ /_____

❑ *What is the best thing about having the*
   size family that we do?

WHAT TO EXPECT

This question will help your child see the positives
about your family size. If the youngest children start
first, there will be considerable variety in what each
family member values about the family size. Children
will compare your family to a smaller family ("we have
people to play with") and to a larger family ("we each
have our own rooms").

Keep the Conversation Going by . . .

Asking your child if she knows other families that are
of different sizes. How are those families like yours?
How are those families different? What would be good
about having a smaller or a larger family? Maybe your
child wouldn't have to share toys or would get more
attention if your family were smaller? Maybe she would
have her choice of babysitters if your family were larger.
What would be a disadvantage to having a smaller or
a larger family?

DATE:_____ /_____ /_____

❑ *What do you do when something doesn't go your way or doesn't go as you expected?*

WHAT TO EXPECT

This is an opportunity for your children to reflect on their coping skills and resiliency. Older family members will talk about very specific things they do when things do not go well and how that helps them. They should answer this question first, modeling for the children how they might respond when things do not go as they want. Kids will then likely talk about feeling frustration at first, but then looking for an alternative solution or switching gears and doing something else.

Keep the Conversation Going by . . .

Asking your child to give you an example of a time when something did not go his way. How did he feel? Was he angry? Upset? Frustrated? Disappointed? How did he respond? Did he yell? Lash out in anger? Accept what was going on? Did his response make the situation better or worse?

DATE:_____ /_____ /_____

❑ *Tell us about a time when you had to make a tough decision.*

WHAT TO EXPECT

Children seldom realize that their parents have had to make tough decisions. Disclosing a particularly tough decision will allow your children to see that you too have had such experiences, and this will give them more confidence when they later face their own tough decisions. A young child's tough decisions will seem trivial to any adolescent at the table. So it might be necessary for the adults at the table to support the younger child as she talks about her tough decision. These tough decisions could involve choosing between two kinds of ice cream, deciding where to sit on the bus, or deciding who to invite to a birthday party.

Keep the Conversation Going by . . .

Encouraging your child to tell you about the different options that were available to him when he had to make this decision. Why did he choose what he chose? How did he make the choice? Does he think he made the right choice? How would the outcome have been different if he had decided to make a different choice?

DATE:_____ /_____ /_____

❑ *If you were to design a ride for an amuse-ment park, what would you want your ride to be like?*

WHAT TO EXPECT

The various rides at amusement parks are fascinating to most children. They are apt to have more interest-ing and unique answers to this question than the adults at the dinner table. You might expect younger kids to design safer sounding rides, but because they are not tall enough to ride the big scary rides at the amuse-ment park, their fantasy is likely to include rides that are fast, tall, and wild. Older kids who have experienced many types of rides will likely describe some that fit their personal preferences.

Keep the Conversation Going by . . .

Asking your child to tell you more about her ride. How old would someone have to be to be allowed to go on this ride? How high up in the air would this ride go? Would it tip people upside down? Would the ride go fast? Would it be scary? Fun? Exciting? What would the ride look like? Would it have a theme? For example, would your child's rollercoaster have a circus theme where the coaster brought the children through flam-ing hoops and a lion's mouth?

DATE:_____ /_____ /_____

❏ *If you could speak to any animal and have it speak back to you, which animal would you choose?*

WHAT TO EXPECT

This is an opportunity for kids to exercise their imaginations and select animals they find fascinating or appealing. If your child has been hooked on a certain type of animal, you can expect that to be the answer. Children are likely to focus on exotic animals they have only encountered in the zoo.

Keep the Conversation Going by . . .

Asking your child what the animal would say. What would he ask the animal? Does he think he would have a lot in common with the animal as they talked? What would the animal's voice sound like? What does he think the animal would want him to know?

DATE: _____ / _____ / _____

❑ *If you were a goldfish, what kinds of things would you want in your fish tank?*

WHAT TO EXPECT

This question will appeal to children who have goldfish or to those who like to look at the fish in pet stores. They may want sea shells in the fish tank, possibly a castle, and rocks with holes big enough that the fish can swim through. Some children might really deck out their tanks with TVs, video games, kitchens, hot tubs, and more. Be sure to give your thoughts about how you would furnish your own fish tank.

Keep the Conversation Going by . . .

Asking your child how he would know if the fish likes those things in its tank. How will the goldfish use those items? Does the goldfish know there is a whole world outside his tank? What does he think about it? Does he dream about visiting other goldfish in their tanks? Does he want to build out and have a bigger tank?

DATE:_____ /_____ /_____

❑ *Think about your favorite fairy tale. Now retell it as a modern story.*

WHAT TO EXPECT

Children will pick a fairy tale that you have likely read to them or told to them and make it fit into their own world. You can expect cars, electronics, modern media, and modern bad guy accessories (like guns) to play a role. Children will enjoy playing with a story they already know and modernizing it to today's world.

Keep the Conversation Going by . . .

Asking your child to tell you how the story ends. Is this a better ending than in the traditional fairy tale? Would it be fun to act out this story? Which role would your child play? Are there other fairy tales she would want to hear retold? How can she tell if something is a fairy tale?

DATE:_____ /_____ /_____

❑ *Is there anything that you know you should do, but you avoid doing as long as you can?*

WHAT TO EXPECT

This question allows all of you to reflect on your capacity for self-discipline and to recognize your tendencies to procrastinate from time to time. Unless you have a highly structured household, most children should be able to think of an activity they avoid doing until the last minute. Their answers might vary from taking a bath, to doing homework, to picking up dirty clothes, to doing chores or walking the dog.

Keep the Conversation Going by . . .

Asking your child why he procrastinates. Is there something about the task that he dislikes? Does he feel that he has better things to do? What are the benefits of putting off this task? What would be the benefits of just getting that task out of the way? What finally gets your child to do that task?

DATE: _____ / _____ / _____

❑ **If you could follow a rainbow, what do you think you would find at the other end?**

WHAT TO EXPECT

If your family has talked about leprechauns and pots of gold, you can expect that as an answer. Children will think about where a rainbow goes and might name other parts of the earth, or they might indulge in some flights of fancy and tell you stories about a make believe land at the other end with things like unicorns and giant flowers. Make up your own story about what you might find at the end.

Keep the Conversation Going by . . .

Asking your child if she would like to go to the end of the rainbow. How long would it take to get there? What happens when the rainbow disappears? Is there rain inside the rainbow? Exactly how long is the rainbow? Can she walk on it like a bridge?

DATE:_____ /_____ /_____

❑ *How do people know when you are happy?*

WHAT TO EXPECT

Looking at someone and being able read their emotions is a valuable social skill and hearing others answer this question will raise your children's awareness of this social skill. Most people at the table will have insight into what they do when they are happy. Your children will probably tell you that they smile when they are happy. They might say they laugh or that they are not crying. They might also associate happiness with doing something fun and might say the person can see them playing.

Keep the Conversation Going by . . .

Asking your child if other people are more likely to see happiness on his face or hear it in his voice. Has there ever been a time when he was happy, but someone read it as a different emotion? What happened? Did he correct that person? How does your child know when you are happy?

DATE:_____ /_____ /_____

❑ *Tell us about a time when you knew something was wrong, but decided to do it anyway.*

WHAT TO EXPECT

Expect to hear some surprising secrets about times your child snuck a cookie, broke something, or did something you had specifically told her not to do. As your children speak, remember that this is not the time to go into lecture mode; rather it is a time to listen, but of course, take note. This is also an opportunity for you to be candid, allowing your children to see that you are more like them than they might have realized.

Keep the Conversation Going by . . .

Encouraging your child to tell you why she decided to do it when she knew it was wrong. How did she feel as she was doing it? Did she feel guilty? Did anyone ever find out that she did it? Is she glad that she did it? If she could turn back the clock, would she do it again? Have there been times where she knew something was wrong and decided not to do it? Have her give an example. Why did she make that decision?

DATE:_____ /_____ /_____

❑ *If you could be any sea creature, which one would you choose?*

WHAT TO EXPECT

Your children are likely to focus on the biggest and most impressive creatures, like whales, dolphins, sharks, or giant squid. Children who have an interest in ocean life might surprise you by choosing offbeat things like sea cucumbers, puffer fish, or clown fish. Everyone at the table can chime in about his or her sea creature of choice.

Keep the Conversation Going by . . .

Asking your child why she chose that creature. What features does she like about it? What does she think that creature does all day? What would it be like to live in the ocean? Would it be scary or fun? What does your child think sea creatures think about life on dry land?

DATE:_____ /_____ /_____

❑ *At what age will you be old?*

WHAT TO EXPECT

Old is always an age that one has not yet reached. For a six-year-old, old might be when she graduates from high school. Don't be surprised if your child picks an age that is younger than you are! Thirty might sound really old to an eight-year-old. For a parent, old might be turning sixty-five. Expect your family members to giggle, laugh, and tease each other over the differences they have in age. This conversation starter will work best if it is asked first to the youngest member of the family and then to the progressively older members of the family.

Keep the Conversation Going by . . .

Asking your child to tell you why that age is old. Who does he think is old? Have him list your family members in order of "oldest" to "youngest." What happens after someone gets old? Is getting old good or bad?

DATE:_____ /_____ /_____

❑ *Name one type of food and one drink that you could not live without.*

WHAT TO EXPECT

You will learn what is important to—or at least enjoyable for—each child in your family. Children will select something that brings them pleasure, perhaps a favorite drink like Coke and a food that they love, like chips or pudding. Older members of the family are apt to select a food that has a lot of nutritional value like salad or something that is habit-forming like coffee.

Keep the Conversation Going by . . .

Asking your child how long has it been since she had that particular food or drink. How much of that food or drink does she have each day? What is it about that food or drink that makes it something she couldn't live without? Is it one of her favorite foods? What would happen if your child really could not live without that particular food or drink and needed to carry it with her every day? How would she carry it? In a bag? Would she invent a magic pill that she could take that tasted like her type of food and drink?

DATE:_____ /_____ /_____

❑ *Why is our family better with you as a member?*

WHAT TO EXPECT

This question helps your child reflect on how he or she contributes to the family. Kids are likely to point out jobs they do such as clearing the table or dusting. They may also focus on fun things they do, like sledding or playing games which they see as important. The roles and contributions of the adults at the dinner table will be obvious to the adults, but spelling them out for the children is a useful exercise. Your children's answers may be surprising as well as insightful.

Keep the Conversation Going by . . .

Having your child tell you if his answer is something he adds to the family every day or just now and then. Does he have to think before he does the things that make him a great family member, or do they come naturally? Ask your child to go around the table and tell each person how he or she contributes and why the family is better with him or her in it.

DATE:_____ /_____ /_____

❑ *Tell us about the biggest prank that any-one in our family has ever pulled.*

WHAT TO EXPECT
This kind of information gives your family history sub-stance and special meaning. It will also help your chil-dren acquire a sense of family tradition. Your children are apt to share surprises, telling about pranks that no one previously knew about.

Keep the Conversation Going by . . .
Encouraging your child to tell you more about the prank. When did it happen? Did anyone there at the time know who had pulled the prank? What happened to the prankster? Ask your child to tell you why that particular prank is his favorite. Why does he think it was such a great prank? What is the best prank he has ever pulled? Was he successful?

DATE: _____ / _____ / _____

❏ *Describe the best fort you have ever built or describe a fort you would like to build.*

WHAT TO EXPECT

Children have a yearning to create a special place that they can call their own. Building a fort is a common experience that everyone can relate to. Children will talk about tents made out of blankets or more permanent wooden structures, depending on what they have experienced. They will also describe fantasy forts they would like to have with lots of amenities built in.

Keep the Conversation Going by . . .

Asking your child why she decided to build this fort. Did she have help? Who helped her? What was the fort made from? Snow? Pillows? Blankets? How long did her fort stay standing? What kinds of fun things did she do for and in her fort? Who was allowed in the fort? What would she do in the imaginary fort she described? How would it be better than any fort she's had before?

DATE:_____ /_____ /_____

❑ *If we were making a photo album about our family, what five pictures would you want to put in it?*

WHAT TO EXPECT

Of course, your child will want to make sure that a picture or two of him is in the family album. Expect your children to want humorous pictures—maybe Mom's backside as she stoops over to get something out of the picnic basket or Dad stepping in a mud puddle as he carries a load of camping stuff from the car. The adults will like more artistic pictures—something with scenery in the background and the subject of the picture looking well composed and picture perfect, or group photos that show the entire family.

Keep the Conversation Going by . . .

Having your child tell you more about the photos he picked. Where were those pictures taken? Who was the photographer? Why does he want them in the family album? Do they mean something special to him? What do the pictures say about your family? After dinner is over, feel free to turn this conversation starter into a family activity by gathering an assortment of family pictures and actually working together to sort through them and make a family album.

DATE:_____ /_____ /_____

❏ *Put a glass on the table. Fill exactly half of it with water. Ask your child if the glass is half full or half empty.*

WHAT TO EXPECT

Children under age eight have likely never heard this before and will scratch their heads. Most are likely to say it is half full. Don't assume that the child who says it is half empty is a pessimist though—he'll blurt out whatever comes to him. Some children will tell you it is both.

Keep the Conversation Going by . . .

Asking your child what the difference is between half full and half empty. Does it feel different to describe the glass one way or the other? Why would your child choose one description over the other? If she were doing homework and had completed exactly half of it, would she say her work was half finished or half unfinished?

DATE:_____ /_____ /_____

❑ *When you become famous, what will you be famous for?*

WHAT TO EXPECT

What child hasn't thought about becoming famous? Children ages five to nine are apt to say that they will become famous for being an actor, singer, or a professional athlete. Older children are already getting a sense of their possible niche in life. So one might say, "I'm going be a famous doctor." Another might say, "I'll be famous for being the first person to walk on Mars." You can talk about what your dreams were as a child for your own famous future.

Keep the Conversation Going by . . .

Asking your child how old he will be when he becomes famous. What are you going to do with your fame? Are you going to make a lot of money when you're famous? How will people know you're famous – will they see you on TV, read about you on the Internet, or hear you on the radio? Do you think that the people who are famous today knew when they were children that they would be famous one day?

DATE:_____ /_____ /_____

❏ *What is the one thing that you've accomplished that you are most proud of?*

WHAT TO EXPECT

Each family member will be able to share and boast about an accomplishment, and other family members will be able to congratulate and encourage them. Children who are eight years old and younger may share an accomplishment that required a motor skill, like learning to ride a bike or roller blade. Older children may name an achievement in a competitive sport or at school. Adults are apt to mention an achievement that took effort over a long duration and persistence.

Keep the Conversation Going by . . .

Encouraging your child to tell you more. Where was she when she accomplished this? Were other people aware of her accomplishment? What did they have to say about what she was able to accomplish? What specifically is she proud of? How much work did she have to do to accomplish this goal? Did anyone help her reach it?

DATE:_____ /_____ /_____

❑ *What makes our family special?*

WHAT TO EXPECT

Expect your children to reflect upon and share things about the family that are special and are a source of pride to them personally. Your children may mention tangible things like how many cats the family has or activities that are important to them, like the fact that everyone can ski. Older people may mention intangible qualities like how supportive everyone is of other family members.

Keep the Conversation Going by . . .

Asking your child if she has, prior to today, ever thought about what makes your family special. What does she think other people think about your family? What does she think makes other families (her cousin's family, her friend's family, etc.) special? Is there one thing that all families share that is special? Have your child tell you what she thinks is special about everyone at the table.

DATE:_____ /_____ /_____

☐ *If you were going to write a letter to the President of the United States, what would it say?*

WHAT TO EXPECT

Expect your children to respond to this conversation starter in one of two ways. They may ask the President for something, as is human nature, or they may want to tell the President something. With a little guidance, your children might tell the President about what they are doing to make their community or their country a better place. Another seldom-seen theme in the hundreds of letters that come to the White House would be a letter expressing appreciation to the President for what he is doing.

Keep the Conversation Going by . . .

Asking your child why she wants to say that in her letter. How does she think the President will feel when he reads her letter? How would she feel if she received a letter like that? If you want to move this conversation beyond talk, encourage everyone to write a letter to the President and read it aloud. You can tell the children that you'll put their letters in the mail and send them to the White House.

DATE:_____ /_____ /_____

❑ *If you had a lot of money and could buy the family three things, what would you buy?*

WHAT TO EXPECT

Although older family members will reflect on how they might contribute to the family, your children won't be so altruistic. Expect your children to mention things that they would enjoy like a new TV, rollerblades, or a trampoline. Don't expect any of them to say, "I'd buy the family a motor home so we could all have lots of space on long trips."

Keep the Conversation Going by . . .

Asking your child why he would buy those things. Who in the family would enjoy using those things? Would those things benefit the family as a whole or certain individuals only? How much money would he need to buy those three things? Would those things still be useful years from now or would the family only be able to use them for a few years? What else would your child buy for the family if money was not a concern?

DATE: _____ / _____ / _____

❑ *If you were to pick a relative to spend the whole day with, which relative would you pick?*

WHAT TO EXPECT

Expect to gain some insight into your children's special bonds with a particular family member. A five-year-old boy might say, "Granddad, because he teaches me how to fish." An eleven-year-old girl might say, "Aunt Carol, so we could go shopping together." An adult might say, "My sister because we like to go for walks and talk together."

Keep the Conversation Going by . . .

Having your child plan out the day he would spend with the relative of his choice. What would he and the relative do? Would they go somewhere or just hang out at home? What would they talk about? Is there any place in particular that your child would like to take this relative? Would he like anyone else to be there or would he like to spend the day alone with the relative? Has your child spent an entire day with that person before? If so, what did they do that day? Would your child like to repeat some of the same things?

DATE:_____ /_____ /_____

❑ *If you were a caveman, what would your day be like?*

WHAT TO EXPECT

Expect your children to be ready to jump in with a lot of stereotypical images involving fur loincloths, caves, and big clubs made out of bones. They'll likely talk about hunting and cooking over a fire. Some younger children might talk about a day involving dinosaurs. You can offer some insight into adult concerns such as worries about safety and finding water.

Keep the Conversation Going by . . .

Asking your child what the hardest thing about being a caveman would be. Where would she sleep if she were a caveman? What would she eat? Would it be cold? What kind of a life does she think caveman children had? Did they go to school? How did they learn things? How were cavemen like us?

DATE: _____ / _____ / _____

❑ *Tell us about the family trip that you remember the best, but is not necessarily your favorite trip.*

WHAT TO EXPECT

The longer and more extensive the family trip, the more likely it is that it left behind a lasting memory with your child. However, while children in the family may remember the same trip, each child will remember things differently about the trip. One person may not remember something that was memorable for someone else. Expect your kids to share about the things that made the trips the most special (or the most awful!).

Keep the Conversation Going by . . .

Encouraging your child to share his memories. How old was he at the time? What does he remember most clearly about that trip? Does anyone else remember that? Has he been to that place more than once? If so, why does this particular vacation stick out for him?

DATE:_____ /_____ /_____

❑ *If you were to make a movie about our town, what would that movie be about?*

WHAT TO EXPECT

You can expect a lot of variety from your children. The first person to answer the question will likely set the direction of the conversation. If the first person talks about using the town as a backdrop for a fictional movie, the conversation will move in that direction. However, if the first person suggests that the movie is a documentary about the town or about some interesting people or annual events that happen in the town, the conversation will probably explore that venue. Kids will focus on the parts of the town they are most involved with—home, school, church, park, and so on.

Keep the Conversation Going by . . .

Having your child describe what the film would be like. Would there be a lot of action? Who would be in the movie? Would the characters be played by people who live in the town or by famous people? Would your child be in the movie? If a famous actress played your child in the movie, who would the role be given to? What songs would be on the movie soundtrack?

DATE:_____ /_____ /_____

❑ *What pictures in your bedroom inspire you?*

WHAT TO EXPECT

When we see something all the time, it is human nature to take it for granted. This question will help your children get in touch with an everyday thing that is important to them. This question will elicit strong responses from your children, who will focus on pictures that tie into current interests, such as a love of a certain cartoon character or an interest in auto racing.

Keep the Conversation Going by . . .

Finding out exactly why that picture is inspirational. Ask your child when she got that picture. Where did it come from? How does it inspire her? Does it make her feel like writing, traveling, doing something she's never done before, etc.? What is it about that particular picture that makes her feel this way? What else does she find inspirational?

DATE:_____ /_____ /_____

❑ *If you could swim in a pool, a lake, or an ocean, which one would you choose?*

WHAT TO EXPECT

Most children will answer based on their experiences. If your son has happy memories of swimming in the lake at Aunt Jen's cottage, that will likely be his answer. Children who have never been to the ocean and who are enraptured with the idea may give that answer. Children over age eight will have definite preferences based on their experiences or impressions. Some children might see pools as being safer, particularly if they have never swum in a lake or ocean.

Keep the Conversation Going by . . .

Asking your child how swimming in each of those three places is different. What does he like about each one? What are the disadvantages of each? Where is the water warmer? Where is it easier to swim? Which one would he like in his own backyard?

DATE: _____ / _____ / _____

❑ *What is the best thing about staying over at someone else's house?*

WHAT TO EXPECT

Children often have sleepovers. This conversation starter will help your children realize what exactly they enjoy about the sleepover. For most children, a sleepover is an adventure to an unknown country. Your children will likely say they like staying up late, since most sleepovers do involve that. Sleepovers also generally have fun elements like movies to watch, snacks to eat, and games to play. Getting to see what life is like at someone else's house is something your child may enjoy. Just interacting with a friend at a time you normally wouldn't is fun in itself for most kids. For adults, staying with someone else for a day or two is a way to get reconnected, but also a way to keep travel costs within the family budget.

Keep the Conversation Going by . . .

Asking your child about the last time she stayed at someone else's house. Whose house did she stay at? Has that person ever stayed overnight at our house? What activities did they do at the sleepover? Did they watch movies? Play games? Did anything change after her friend's parents went to bed? Did she have more fun when it was just her and her friend? If she hosted a sleepover, what would she like to do?

DATE:_____ /_____ /_____

❑ *Tell us about two different chores around the house that you would consider doing, which you do not normally do now.*

WHAT TO EXPECT

People tend to get stuck in routines and do the same things day after day without really thinking that they could be doing other tasks. That routine is okay if you love the tasks that you're doing, but it is not okay when you don't. Asking this question will get your children thinking that it might just be possible to shed jobs and tasks that they don't like and take on new or different responsibilities. Children are likely to pick jobs they perceive as easier than the ones they currently do. They may choose tasks that they are not old enough to do and consequently think sound like fun, such as mowing the lawn or doing the grocery shopping.

Keep the Conversation Going by . . .

Encouraging your child to tell you about the advantages of doing one of these different chores. Would doing a different chore be fun? What would be the disadvantages or doing a different chore? Would it take a while to learn how to do the new chore successfully? Is there any one chore or task that your child is especially interested in learning about? Maybe she wants to learn how to cook or wants to babysit a younger sibling?

DATE:_____ /_____ /_____

❑ *What do you like to do on a rainy day?*

WHAT TO EXPECT

Many people don't seize the moment. Instead, they let daily responsibilities direct then one way or another. It will be useful for your children to think about using bad weather as an opportunity to do an interesting thing. You and the other adults at the table have seen many rainy days, making you experienced at taking advantage of a day that disrupts the usual agenda. So you should be the first to answer this question so your children can see the wide range of possible answers to this question. Children will focus on fun activities such as playing games, baking cookies, or doing science experiments.

Keep the Conversation Going by . . .

Explaining the meaning of the term "save it for a rainy day" to your child. Ask him why he thinks people save things for a rainy day. Has he ever put activities aside so he would have them to do on a rainy day? What did he do during the last rainy day? How does he feel about rainy days? Does he like them? Dislike them? Do his feelings change depending on the time of year? Is a rainy day in the summer different than a rainy day in the fall? Why?

DATE:_____ /_____ /_____

❑ *What would be the most difficult thing to eat if a knife was your only utensil?*

WHAT TO EXPECT

This conversation starter will get your whole family laughing together at the answers that are given. Whatever the first person names, chances are the next person will top it. Your family will be drawn into a flurry of foods difficult to eat with a knife and your children will hone directly in on some of the hardest things, such as ice cream or pudding.

Keep the Conversation Going by . . .

Asking your child to show you how eating that food with just a knife would look. How long would it take for her to eat it? Are there any foods that are impossible to eat with just a knife? What foods would be difficult to eat with only a fork or only a spoon? Why would they be so difficult?

DATE:_____ /_____ /_____

❑ *If you could smell like any one thing all the time, what would you choose?*

WHAT TO EXPECT

Expect your kids to try for some laughs by offering some inappropriate responses. Their serious answers will focus on smells they each particularly enjoy. Sweet-smelling fragrances will be offered up. Enticing food smells may be popular. You might hear some interesting responses, such as a child who wants to smell like a dog, finger paint, or dirt.

Keep the Conversation Going by . . .

Asking why that smell appeals to your child. What would other people think if he smelled like that? Does he think he would get tired of smelling that way? If he made a perfume with this smell, what would he call it? Does a person's smell affect what your child thinks of him or her? Who does your child know that smells good?

DATE:_____ /_____ /_____

❑ *Where do you think people go after they die?*

WHAT TO EXPECT

If your family has taught a religion to your children, answers will likely mirror the teachings of the religion. Note that for children over age ten, this may open the door for them to admit that they have a different belief than the one they've been taught. Some children might answer the question literally and respond with "a grave." Remember that the purpose of the conversation is for everyone to freely share their views without being told they are wrong. The interesting part of the conversation will be how your children describe that place or state of being. This is a good opportunity for you to jump in with your own visions and ideas of what happens after death.

Keep the Conversation Going by . . .

Asking your child what it would be like there. What do people do? What do they wear? What does it smell like? Who is in charge? Do people have fun? Is there furniture? Do the seasons change? How would someone get there? How does she know this is what it is like?

DATE: _____ / _____ / _____

❑ *Thirty years ago there weren't any micro-*
waves, iPods, or desktop computers. Thirty
years from now, what do you think most
families will have that has not yet been
invented?

WHAT TO EXPECT

This conversation starter requires your children to think outside of the box and look into the future. You may be surprised to see that your youngest children might just be able to display the most flexible thinking, coming up with things that would be useful but are now thought to be impossible. Older children will come up with more advanced computers and electronics that do things current machines cannot.

Keep the Conversation Going by . . .

Encouraging your child to tell you more about her invention. Does she see a need for this particular item? What will people do with it? What do people have to do now since this item isn't yet available? How would she market this item? What color would it be? Would it be big or small? How much would it cost?

DATE:_____ /_____ /_____

❑ *What would happen if it snowed inside our home?*

WHAT TO EXPECT

Expect your children to focus on the positives with this question. Snowballs, snow forts, snowmen, and indoor sled runs are likely to come to mind. Once an older member of the family points out some negative consequences, they will shift their thinking and realize it would be cold and hard to move around.

Keep the Conversation Going by . . .

Asking what might make it snow inside. How would your child have to dress? What could your family do to clean up the snow? What would happen if it melted? If your child made a snowman, which room would he put it in? In which room would he like an ice skating rink? How does he think you would react if you came home and found the house filled with snow?

DATE: _____ / _____ / _____

❑ *What are three things that you'd change about your school?*

WHAT TO EXPECT

It's human nature to see things that could be better. So everyone at the dinner table will have ideas about what could be changed. The first answers will involve making school more fun—no homework, more recess, no tests, and so on. You can help to steer the conversation to other types of changes your child would like made to the actual school itself or the way things are done there.

Keep the Conversation Going by . . .

Encouraging your child to tell you why she chose those three particular things. Are they causes close to her heart? For example, does she want the school auditorium or gymnasium to be updated because she is interested in theater or sports? What would it take to change that? Why does she think someone hasn't changed it already?

DATE:_____ /_____ /_____

❑ *If you had to live without vision, hearing, taste, touch, or smell, which would you pick?*

WHAT TO EXPECT

This conversation starter will force your children to think through the benefits of the five senses and weigh their value. It will also help them to understand the perspectives of those who do have a disability. It will take a few minutes for your kids to think through the options. They might choose taste or smell since they could think they could still function almost normally without them, but they may come up with some excellent rationales for choosing another sense.

Keep the Conversation Going by . . .

Asking your child why he chose that sense. How would his life be different without it? What changes would he have to make in the way he lives? Which of the senses does he think is the most important? Why? What must life have been like for Helen Keller who was both blind and deaf?

DATE:_____ /_____ /_____

❏ *If you got to choose a game for a family game night, what game would you choose?*

WHAT TO EXPECT

Your child may choose her favorite game or pick one that the family has not played in a long time. Your child could name a game she associates with family together-ness or games that need a lot of players to make them fun, such as Twister. Make sure everyone answers the question—you included! Your child may want to play the game she picked after dinner, or ask when you could have a family game night and play the games everyone has named.

Keep the Conversation Going by . . .

Asking your child why she chose that game. Is it her favorite? If so, why? What does she like about it? Who usually wins when the family plays that game? Does your child think she can beat other family members when playing that particular game? How long will it take to play that game? If your child could invent her own board game, what existing game would it be like? What would the premise be? How could the game be won?

DATE:_____ /_____ /_____

❑ *What would you wear if you were asked to dress in a way that represented a country or area of your family's origin?*

WHAT TO EXPECT

This conversation starter will force your children to think about their culture and this presents a good opportunity to talk about the family's ancestral roots. It will be interesting to let the children in the family go first in order to get some insight into how well they understand their family's origins. If they do understand where your family came from, they may not have any real understanding of how people from that area dress, but you can bet they will come up with some suggestions hinged on what they do know about the area (for example if they know your family is from Peru, they might suggest clothes made from llama fur). The adults in the family can then follow up with a historically accurate awareness of the family's country of origin and the type of dress that typifies that area.

Keep the Conversation Going by . . .

Having your child think about how she would look if she dressed up in that outfit. Has she ever seen anyone wear anything like that? How does she think she would look wearing that? How would she feel while wearing it? Proud of her heritage? Embarrassed to be wearing something so different from what she would normally wear?

DATE:_____ /_____ /_____

❑ *If you were to make a chalk drawing on our driveway that represents our family, what would your drawing look like?*

WHAT TO EXPECT

Most children will think of an image that literally shows each family member and might include pets. You can encourage them to think outside the box by asking them to describe a drawing that doesn't just have drawings of each of you, but shows things that somehow represent your family. Share your own ideas about what you would draw.

Keep the Conversation Going by . . .

Asking your child why he would create that drawing. How would those images represent the family? What about the family would he try to get across? What colors would the drawing be? Why would he choose those colors? Would certain colors represent certain people or certain things about our family? What does he think the neighbors will say about that drawing?

DATE:_____ / _____ / _____

❑ *If you invented a brand new sport, what would it be?*

WHAT TO EXPECT

Expect your children younger than ten to need a little time to think this conversation starter over. They may have a difficult time thinking of a brand new sport at first. As the facilitator, you might want to be the first family member to answer the question and then move chronologically down the family structure. This strategy will model plausible answers that will get your children's imaginations churning. You will hear some pretty insane suggestions, but just accept them as offered. Don't be surprised if your children come up with sports that sound impossible (such as kicking a ball up into outer space) or have rules or components that don't make a lot of sense (like the first person to sit down on the kangaroo wins, but the second person has to sit on a tortoise, but only if the aardvark isn't nearby).

Keep the Conversation Going by . . .

Having your child tell you the details of her new sport. Is it a team sport or an individual sport? Would your family be able to play this sport together? What existing sport does it most resemble? What equipment would she need to play this sport? What are the rules of the sport? Would it be something she'd like to watch on TV? Offer details about the sport that you made up as well. Talk about whose sport everyone would like to try.

DATE:_____ /_____ /_____

❑ *Tell about a time when a friend hurt you.*

WHAT TO EXPECT

People sometimes harbor hurtful feelings, which can damage relationships. People are also sometimes hurt by things that another person did totally by accident, but if they could get some objectivity, they would understand the broader perspective and be able to resolve their feelings. However, these realizations cannot happen unless they are aired in a safe environment—for your children, that safe environment can be your dinner table. It is likely that your children will share a hurt that has festered. Just talking about their feelings will help them work toward resolving the issue.

Keep the Conversation Going by . . .

Encouraging your child to tell you more about her hurt. When did this happen? Was it yesterday or a long time ago? Is she still friends with the person who hurt her? Does she think the person hurt her on purpose? How did she react when this person hurt her? Can she think of a time when she may have hurt someone's feelings? How did she feel knowing that she hurt someone else? How did she resolve that issue?

DATE: _____ / _____ / _____

❏ *If you were going to travel across the United States, would you rather go by train, by motorcycle, or by RV?*

WHAT TO EXPECT

Expect to hear an interesting conversation about your children's different perspectives and preferences and what they might want to see most when traveling. Some children might think a train is exotic and fun— particularly children who have played with trains. Other children might think a motorcycle sounds dangerous and fun. Other children might think the idea of an RV is fun because they would be able to sleep and play in it.

Keep the Conversation Going by . . .

Asking your child how she thinks her trip would be different if she went across the country in one of these different ways. Would she see different things? Meet different people? Experience her trip in a different way? What would she want to see on her trip? Does she have a destination in mind? Which would be the fastest way to travel?

DATE:_____ /_____ /_____

❑ *Tell us about the wackiest cake you can think of making for your birthday.*

WHAT TO EXPECT

This conversation starter will get your children to stretch their imaginations and fantasize about that most exciting childhood event—the birthday. Children will make their cakes wackier and crazier as the conversation moves along. Don't be surprised if they become completely unrealistic!

Keep the Conversation Going by . . .

Encouraging your child to use his imagination. What color frosting would he put on his cake? Would he use more than one color? What shape would he make his cake? How many layers tall would his cake be? Would he even be able to bring it into the house? What flavors would his cake be? Normal flavors like vanilla or chocolate, or crazy flavors like macaroni and cheese or chicken nuggets? Would there be decorations on the cake? What would the decorations look like?

DATE:_____ /_____ /_____

❑ *If you live in the city, in the country, or in the suburbs, what would change if you moved to one of the other two areas?*

WHAT TO EXPECT

Where you live has a powerful influence on your life. This question will challenge your children to consider how a change in environment would impact them. Your children will show the most enthusiasm for the hypothetical move, thinking of all of the novel things to explore. The answer your child gives will help you gain some insight into things she longs for or wants to experience. The adults at the table may be more pragmatic; their first question is likely to be, "What kind of work would I do?"

Keep the Conversation Going by . . .

Asking your child if she would like the changes a move would facilitate. What would the advantages be to living in one of the other areas? The disadvantages? Would she really want to move? What would she miss about where you live now if your family really did move?

DATE:_____ / _____ / _____

❑ *What would life be like if we slept during the day and were awake during the night?*

WHAT TO EXPECT

Your children will be excited by this question because it lets them consider breaking all the rules! Not having to go to bed at the traditional bedtime will be quite appealing. They will likely think it sounds really neat at first, but as everyone talks, they may come to see the disadvantages. They'll think about not being able to play outside and how dark it would always be.

Keep the Conversation Going by . . .

Asking your child if it would be hard to sleep when it is light out. Would your family use more energy for electricity if you were only awake at night? What kinds of activities would be difficult or impossible to do? Would your child miss seeing the sun? What changes would he need to make to his life? What would school be like at night?

DATE: _____ / _____ / _____

❑ *If everyone in our family had to dress alike in one way for our family reunion, what would we wear?*

WHAT TO EXPECT

Expect your children to want everyone to wear to something outlandish, such as feathered masks, super hero capes, or face paint. The adults may suggest modest, inconspicuous attire like a ball cap or common T-shirt. Since it is unlikely that everyone will come up with the same idea, the family will have to compromise.

Keep the Conversation Going by . . .

Asking your child why he thinks you should all wear that particular item. How will it make you stand out from the other families? What would your child like the other families to wear? Something similar? Something totally different? Should your family do this sometime just for fun? Where would your child want your family to go when you were all dressed alike?

DATE:_____ /_____ /_____

❑ *Tell us about a time when you told some-one a secret, but they didn't keep it.*

WHAT TO EXPECT

Some secrets are benign, like planning a surprise birth-day party. However, some secrets are best kept until the right circumstances are put in place for sharing the information, like a conversation between parents about a life-threatening illness or the impending loss of a job. So the answers to this question are apt to range from humorous to tragic. Your child may talk about a time she told a friend that she liked a boy and the friend told someone else, which can be highly embarrassing for elementary-school children. There may be discussion of secrets not kept between siblings at the table, such as when your son told your daughter not to tell you he did something.

Keep the Conversation Going by . . .

Encouraging your child to tell you more about the situ-ation. What happened when his secret was not kept? How did he feel? Angry? Frustrated? Betrayed? Did something negative happen as a result? What did he learn from that? If he could do the whole thing over again, would he do anything differently?

DATE:_____ /_____ /_____

❏ *What is the best thing about eating out?*

WHAT TO EXPECT

You will learn about everyone's eating out favorites. Most children have eaten away from home, so everyone can join in this conversation. The adults get to choose when the family eats out, so they will probably mention the convenience of having a day off from cooking. Your children in the five to seven age range will likely name fast food favorites, particularly if your family rarely goes to those restaurants and they are considered a special treat. Your older children may mention restaurants that have their favorite meal (of the moment!) and may name Mexican, Italian, or Chinese restaurants.

Keep the Conversation Going by . . .

Telling your child what you love about eating out and then asking him for more details about his experiences. How does he decide what to order in a restaurant? Did he ever order something he wished he hadn't? Does he have a favorite dish that he orders every time he goes to a particular restaurant? If so, what is it and why does he like it so much? Would he rather go out to eat or eat at home? What is the difference? If he could open up his own restaurant what kind would he open? What type of food would he serve?

DATE: _____ / _____ / _____

❑ *If you could learn to speak a second language, which would you choose?*

WHAT TO EXPECT

Children find other languages fascinating and may have
had exposure through your community or through TV.
Your younger children may choose something that sounds
very exotic to them, such as Chinese. Your children who
are closer to age eleven may already be thinking about
taking a second language in middle school or high school
and may have formed some realistic opinions about this.

Keep the Conversation Going by . . .

Asking why that language appeals to your child. Does
she think it would be easier to speak than English?
Does she want to know more about the culture and
country where the language is spoken? Does she know
any words in that language? Does she know anyone
who speaks that language? Why would it be useful to
learn another language?

DATE:_____ /_____ /_____

❑ *If you could choose to never brush your teeth, wash your hair, or cut your nails ever again, which would you choose and why?*

WHAT TO EXPECT

The thought of getting to completely ignore a grooming task will likely be quite exciting to your children in the five to seven age range. Your children who are particularly resistant to regular self-care will jump on board this one quickly. Children over age eight may be horrified at the thought of this, because peer pressure about appearances becomes quite active around this age.

Keep the Conversation Going by . . .

Asking your child how it would feel to live with one of these body parts ungroomed. Would other people notice? What would they think? How might daily activities become more difficult? What could he do to cover up the problem or distract people from the lack of grooming?

DATE:_____ /_____ /_____

❏ *How would you describe yourself in five words or less?*

WHAT TO EXPECT

Expect your children to describe themselves with five positive words that tell about their physical characteristics and attributes like strong, fast, tall, skinny, etc., because these are the characteristics that children are most focused on—the physical and visual. They are most tuned into how people look and haven't yet learned to be as aware of inner characteristics, at least not in ways they can verbalize quickly. Adolescents will describe themselves in five words that tell how they hope they are perceived by their peers: cool, hip, smart, nice, etc. The adults at the table will describe themselves in five words that tell about their core values: honest, dependable, industrious, etc.

Keep the Conversation Going by . . .

Asking your child if she thinks those same five words will describe her five years from now. If not, what words will? What is another word that her friends might suggest adding to this list? Have everyone in your family go around the table and describe everyone else in five words or less. This will help your family members see how others view them.

DATE:_____ /_____ /_____

❏ *What does it mean to make a promise?*

WHAT TO EXPECT

Your children will jump in with talk about saying something and then doing it and will offer some examples such as promising to have a play date with a friend, an adult promising dessert, and so on. They will focus on promises that have to do with activities and material rewards since those are the kinds of promises that are most important in their life. You can talk about other kinds of promises, such as marriage vows, promises of loyalty, and the meaning of 'giving your word' to someone.

Keep the Conversation Going by . . .

Asking your child why promises are important. How does he feel when someone breaks a promise? Has he ever broken a promise? What did he do? Did he apologize? Can he trust someone if they break a promise? Should he be careful about what kinds of promises he makes?

DATE:_____ /_____ /_____

❏ *If you could pick what the weather would be like tomorrow, what would you choose?*

WHAT TO EXPECT

If you live in a climate where something like snow or very hot days are a rarity, expect your children to choose that for the novelty factor. Children who love to do outdoors activities will likely choose a weather forecast that suits their activities. A rare child will choose a rainy day, but may have a very good reason for it if she does—because she likes to stay inside and play games with you or enjoys baking cookies as a rainy day activity.

Keep the Conversation Going by . . .

Asking your child what it would be like if she got to choose the weather all the time. What would happen if no one ever picked a rainy day? How would your child present her weather forecast if she were on TV? What would it be like if every family got to pick the weather for their little area?

DATE:_____ /_____ /_____

❏ *When you look at yourself in the mirror, what is the first thing you look at?*

WHAT TO EXPECT

Younger children will likely respond with a general answer such as "my face." You can ask your child to be more detailed and can expect answers like "my eyes" or "my mouth." The older the child, the more focused he or she is likely to be on things like hair or skin, which start to become an issue after age eight or nine.

Keep the Conversation Going by . . .

Asking your child how often she looks at herself in a mirror. How does she feel about the first thing she sees when she views herself? Is she proud? Frustrated? Embarrassed? Does she think other people focus on the same thing she sees when they look at her? Have your child tell each person at the table about the first thing she sees when she looks at them.

TAKE A TIP:
MAKE FAMILY CELEBRATIONS
A TRADITION

Home is more than a place where you eat and sleep; it is a place where families can make memories and affirm what matters most. There are abundant opportunities for family celebrations. The less common celebrations of everyday milestones can be particularly meaningful because they represent a personal achievement. For example, when our daughter was two years old, my mother bought our family a red dinner plate that was accompanied by an indelible marker for recording family history on the plate. The plate was to be used on special occasions to honor a family member's achievement.

Our daughter came to love Red Plate dinners. She enjoyed reading and re-reading the history of family accomplishments. Early entries for her included when she learned "cursive writing," rode her two-wheeled bicycle for the first time, swam across the pool without her water wings, passed her addition and subtraction test in the allotted five minutes, and scored a goal in soccer. We could tell that even in her teen years, she valued these family celebrations. There was an occasional proclamation, "Guess what happened today. Get out the Red Plate for dinner!"

So don't wait for a holiday or a special occasion. Instead, take the time to celebrate the little things and make dinner time special every day. Your children will thank you for it!

DATE:_____ /_____ /_____

❑ *Tell us about a time when you apologized for something you did.*

WHAT TO EXPECT

Your children will get to be on equal footing with you, since everyone at the table has had this experience. Expect your children to tell you about a fairly recent circumstance when they had to apologize. The adults will dredge back in their memory to find such an experience, but it will be more poignant.

Keep the Conversation Going by . . .

Encouraging your child to tell you more about the apology. Who did he apologize to? What did he apologize for? At the time, did he think he had done something wrong? Does he really think he did something wrong now or did he only apologize because he felt he had to? Looking back on it, does he now think that what he did could have been handled a different way?

DATE:_____ /_____ /_____

❑ *If you had trouble completing a project, what are three things that you would do?*

WHAT TO EXPECT

Your children will probably give weak answers to this question. That is to be expected. Your children may say they would ask you or a teacher for help, since that is their first line of attack in these situations. Problem solving is an acquired skill. Some of the most successful people are successful not because they know the solutions to many problems. Rather, they are successful because they know how to find the solution to the problem. This conversation will give you an opportunity to model that skill for your children.

Keep the Conversation Going by . . .

Asking your child if she has ever had trouble completing a project. Was this frustrating? Did she feel confident that she could solve the problem? What did she do? What helped her the most when she was stuck? If she did complete the project, how did she feel afterwards?

DATE:_____ /_____ /_____

❑ *What is the weirdest or strangest thing
that happened to you this week?*

WHAT TO EXPECT

Expect your children to have a story to tell because
something strange or unusual happens every week
to nearly everyone. Perhaps someone said something
really stupid in class or the cooks at school served
a really horrible pizza. They may not have something
earth shaking, or something that will be remembered
forever, but they will have something to say.

Keep the Conversation Going by . . .

Asking your child to tell you more. Where did this happen? What did he do? Did anyone else think this was
strange or weird? What is the strangest thing that has
ever happened to him? Have him tell you about it. Be
sure to share your stories as well!

DATE:_____ /_____ /_____

❏ *If you were going to be a statue for a day,
who or what would you be?*

WHAT TO EXPECT

You will be able to assess your child's awareness of
the bigger world and some of things in it. Your children
could pick an already existing statue—it might be a
statue of an animal instead of a human—that they have
seen in their community. They could choose a person
or animal to be that they have not seen as an actual
statue. Most kids have some experience with acting like
a statue, or freezing during a game. Older children and
adults will draw from a wider range of experiences to
select a statue, and may select a statue of someone
they admire.

Keep the Conversation Going by . . .

Having your child tell you about her statue in detail.
How would she pose? Who does she think will stop
to look at her? How will she feel when birds land on
her? How did she get to be a statue in the first place?
Would a genie or a witch turn her into a statue? How
would she break the spell and become a person again?
Would there be advantages to being a statue? Maybe
people would admire her or stop to take pictures.
Would there be disadvantages? How would it feel to
hold perfectly still for an entire day?

DATE:_____ /_____ /_____

❑ *If you were going to travel across an ocean, would you rather go in a sailboat, on a cruise ship, or in an airplane?*

WHAT TO EXPECT

Your children's answers may be determined by what they've actually done. A child who has been in a plane may pick something else because it is new. A child who loves boats may pick the sailboat since it fits with her interests. You will also probably get a sense of what is important to each child when they travel, whether it be adventure, comfort, or getting there quickly.

Keep the Conversation Going by . . .

Asking your child to describe why she would like to travel that way. What are the benefits of choosing that option? Why might someone else want to go a different way? Where is your child going on this trip? How long will she stay? Will she come home via the same mode of transportation on which she left or would she like to try something different?

DATE:_____ /_____ /_____

❑ *In school, who or what decides whether someone is popular?*

WHAT TO EXPECT

This conversation starter will help you gain insight into your child's adjustment to school and whether he feels accepted. For children, popularity is often determined by the assessment of others. Your child will likely tell you that other kids decide who is popular, and they may say that the kids who are already popular choose who else will be popular. If your child sees herself as unpopular there may be some emotion in this conversation since she might be feeling left out or puzzled by her lack of acceptance.

Keep the Conversation Going by . . .

Asking your child if she feels that is a good way to determine popularity. If not, how does she think popularity should be determined? Who are some of the popular kids in her school? How does she feel about them? Does she feel that she is popular? Tell your child about your school years. Were you popular? How did you deal with that?

DATE: _____ / _____ / _____

❑ *What would your life be like if you only did the things that you wanted to do and never did the things you didn't want to do?*

WHAT TO EXPECT

This conversation starter is designed to help children understand the importance of being mindful of daily responsibilities and how they impact others. An adult at the table should answer this question first, keeping his or her comments focused on his or her life and responsibilities. For example, you could say, "Some days I'd like to sleep in and get to work an hour or two late. But if I did that, I'd probably lose my job." At first children will imagine a perfect life if they only did the things they wanted to, but as the conversation progresses they will think more about the consequences of those actions and how that would affect them.

Keep the Conversation Going by . . .

Asking your child what might happen if he actually lived his life in that way. Would he like the consequences that followed those decisions? What would those consequences be? How would those decisions affect the other members of the family? Give your child specific examples to think about. For example, what would happen if he didn't clear his plate off the table? Would it sit there for months, growing mold and becoming smelly? Would someone else have to do it for him? Would that person resent having to do that?

DATE:_____ /_____ /_____

❏ *Do you care what other people think about you?*

WHAT TO EXPECT

The answers will give you insight into your child's social judgment and understanding. Children usually care about what other people (their peers) think because it means having friends. They also generally want to be liked by their teachers. You might want to talk about how as an adult you want other people to respect you, but that the most important thing is what you think of yourself.

Keep the Conversation Going by . . .

Asking your child why he cares what people think. Does he intentionally do things to make other people think well of him? Are there some things that he doesn't do to make other people think well of him? Are there things he wishes he could do, but doesn't because he's afraid of what others may think? What does he think would happen if he did something that others wouldn't like?

DATE: _____ / _____ / _____

❏ *If you could switch places with anyone at this table for the day tomorrow, whom would you pick?*

WHAT TO EXPECT

Your children will pick someone older at the table. The idea of being an adult or a teenager for the day will be quite appealing because your child assumes there is more freedom. The thought of being in charge of himself and doing whatever he wants will seem wonderful. He won't immediately think about the responsibilities that come with age.

Keep the Conversation Going by . . .

Asking your child what he thinks would be the best part of living that person's day. Would he like to go to that person's job or school? How would he feel doing that person's household responsibilities? What would be the hardest thing about being that person for a day? What would your child miss about his own regular life?

DATE: _____ / _____ / _____

❑ *If your best friend moved away to another state, how would you stay in touch with him?*

WHAT TO EXPECT

The thought of a good friend moving away might be hard, particularly if your child has already experienced this. Most children will be optimistic about this and believe that they really could remain best friends despite the move. They may talk about sending e-mail (children closer to eleven might mention texts), talking on the phone, writing letters, visiting each other, or using Internet technology such as Skype to see and talk to each other through the computer.

Keep the Conversation Going by . . .

Asking your child what he thinks would be the hardest part of having a good friend move away. How might calling and emailing help the friend adjust to the move? What kinds of things would she talk to her friend about after he moved? Would she find another best friend after he moved? How often would your child want to visit her friend after the move?

DATE: _____ / _____ / _____

❑ *What does it mean to be smart?*

WHAT TO EXPECT

Your child will most likely immediately think of academic success and relate this question only to school. Depending on how your child feels about school, she might not see herself as smart. You can talk about all the kinds of things people can be smart about and widen your child's understanding of this concept.

Keep the Conversation Going by . . .

Asking your child how she thinks people become smart. Are they born that way or do they have to work at it? What kinds of things is she smart at? Are there things she wishes she was smarter about? Who is the smartest person she knows? Does she think she has to be the smartest person at something to be good at it?

DATE:_____/_____/_____

❑ *What is your favorite month of the year and why?*

WHAT TO EXPECT

You can expect your children to choose December if you celebrate Christmas or Hanukkah, the months of their birthdays, or the first month off from school in the summer, because they are focused on direct benefits to themselves. You might widen the discussion by talking about the month with the best weather, or the month that you find the most relaxing (which might be one completely devoid of holidays and big events!).

Keep the Conversation Going by . . .

Suggesting your child think what it might be like to have Christmas or Hanukkah in a different month. Would that month then be his favorite? What if his birthday was in a different month? Which month would he pick for his birthday if he could choose? Would these celebrations feel different if they happened at different times of the year? Would they be more or less fun at other times of the year?

DATE:_____ /_____ /_____

❑ *What do kids know more about than adults?*

WHAT TO EXPECT

This conversation starter offers the children in your family the opportunity to take center stage. Expect them to become animated and gleeful telling about the things that they know more about than you. Video games may be at the top of their list. They may list TV shows, board games, or sports they know more about than you do. If your child sees himself as very knowledgeable about something he's really into, like sharks or horses, that might be another answer that will come up.

Keep the Conversation Going by . . .

Having your child tell you why she thinks kids know more about that particular thing than parents. Is that something adults should try to learn? What does she think adults know more about than kids? Does she think that she'll learn that thing when she gets older? Is there anything your child knows more about than other kids? Why does she think this is?

DATE:_____ /_____ /_____

❑ *If an astronaut said he would take you on a trip into outer space if you could give him good reasons to take you, what reasons would you give?*

WHAT TO EXPECT

Every child at the dinner table will be excited about boarding a space shuttle for a trip into space, and they will try to come up with good reasons for why they should be given a free trip. They may need to think to come up with some reasons, and might say they could help steer the ship, would take up less space than another adult, or because they know a lot about stars.

Keep the Conversation Going by . . .

Having your child tell you why he would want to go into outer space. Would he want to experience weightlessness? Would he want to walk on the moon? Would he want to check out the space station? What does he think Earth would look like from way out in space? Would he be somewhat scared? Would he be lonely? Would he want to take anyone with him? What would he pack if he were going into space? How would he make sure the contents of his suitcase didn't fly all over the space shuttle when his bag was opened? Would he have to tie everything down?

DATE:_____ / _____ / _____

❑ *Clip a news article from the newspaper (making sure it is age appropriate) and read the first paragraph. Ask "Why do you think that happened or what do you think will happen?"*

WHAT TO EXPECT

Expect your children to consider current events, the reasons for them, and the impact of the events on others. The question will help expand the range of issues your family normally talks about. This is a particularly good question to ask after something challenging has happened that turned the family attention inward, such as moving or losing a pet.

Keep the Conversation Going by . . .

Encouraging your child to tell you how he feels about the story you just read. Did it make him happy? Sad? Excited? Scared? Does he think that what happened was fair? How does he think people will cope with what happened?

DATE:_____ /_____ /_____

❑ *If you were the family chef for the eve-*
ning and everyone wanted pizza, what
wild and crazy toppings would you
choose?

WHAT TO EXPECT

Your child will likely start by listing her own favorite
topping. You can then expect to hear of some pizza toppings that you never even thought were possible as the
conversation moves along. You might hear chocolate
chips, jelly beans, cookies, and so on. As the conversation goes from one person to the next, the ideas will
get increasingly crazy.

Keep the Conversation Going by . . .

Asking your child what she thinks such a pizza would
taste like. Would it be good? Does she think anyone
would be interested in eating it? Would there be something special that would have to be done with the pizza
before it was eaten? Would it still need to be cooked?
Would it be topped with whipped cream or dipped in
chocolate? Would your child like to try to make such
a pizza?

DATE:_____ /_____ /_____

❏ *If you were to do volunteer work in our community, what would you volunteer to do and why?*

WHAT TO EXPECT

Many children do not know that there are organizations in the community that rely on volunteers. So you may have to tell them that agencies and programs such as animal shelters, food pantries, soup kitchens, or Meals on Wheels need people to help out. Your child will likely focus on an organization which appeals to his interests. Animal shelters are likely to be a popular idea. Volunteering takes time, and requires a willingness to give of one's time, something the adults will likely realize, but the children will not.

Keep the Conversation Going by . . .

Having your child tell you more about how she feels about volunteering. What kind of work does she think she would do there? Why would she choose that type of work? What about it does she think she would enjoy? Is there anything she thinks she would dislike? After talking about volunteering at that agency, does she have any interest in seeing whether she could actually volunteer there?

DATE: _____ / _____ / _____

❑ *What is the neatest magic trick you have seen?*

WHAT TO EXPECT
Most children love magic tricks and this question will give them an opportunity to talk about an area of interest. Expect your children to become animated talking about a particular magic trick that has captured their attention, most likely one that they cannot find any explanation for at all.

Keep the Conversation Going by . . .
Asking your child where he saw this magic trick performed. Who performed it? How does he think it was done? Was it magic or some other sleight of hand? What does he think the trick actually is? Would he like to learn to do a magic trick? How does he think magicians learn magic? Is there a school they go to? A book they read?

DATE: _____ / _____ / _____

❑ *If you were to throw a surprise party, who would you like to surprise?*

WHAT TO EXPECT

Expect your family members to think about what they can do to bring a bit of joy to someone else. Your children will likely suggest throwing a surprise birthday party for a friend. Older family members are apt to suggest a surprise party for a favorite relative.

Keep the Conversation Going by . . .

Encouraging your child to tell you more about the surprise party. What would be the occasion? Would the party have a theme? Who would your child invite? What types of food and drinks would she serve? Where would she hold the surprise party? At your house? At a restaurant? How would she reveal the surprise? Would she have everyone hide and jump out at the unsuspecting person? Would she surprise them in a different way? Does your child think that she would enjoy a surprise party?

DATE:_____ /_____ /_____

❑ *If you joined the circus, what job would you want to do?*

WHAT TO EXPECT

Your young child will choose a circus job he finds exciting or glamorous, such as lion taming or fire eating. Children over age eight are likely to give it some serious thought and pick a job they think they could actually do. Children who have some kind of experience in areas that are similar to circus performing (such as gymnastics or horseback riding) may choose jobs that rely on those talents.

Keep the Conversation Going by . . .

Asking your child why he picked that job. What would be fun about it? What might be hard? Would he enjoy being in front of the audience? Are there jobs at the circus he could do that are behind the scenes? What would it be like to travel around with a circus and be in a different city every week? What would it smell like backstage at the circus? Would he like seeing the clowns take off their makeup? What kinds of things would he eat if he worked at the circus?

DATE:_____ /_____ /_____

❑ *Make up a story about how someone invented the vacuum cleaner.*

WHAT TO EXPECT

Everyone will get an opportunity to hone his or her skills at becoming a good storyteller. Expect your children to tell the most elaborate, creative stories. Your child might imagine that a person saw an elephant pick up something with his trunk and that was the beginning of the idea. She might talk about someone sucking something up through a straw, which led to the concept.

Keep the Conversation Going by . . .

Encouraging your child to give more details. Why did someone invent the vacuum cleaner? What did the inventor need to vacuum up? If there was dirt on the floor why didn't he or she use a broom? How does your child think the inventor figured out how a vacuum cleaner should work? Does she think the inventor got it right the first time or did the person have to try a few times before he or she got it right? What would life be like without a vacuum cleaner?

DATE:_____ /_____ /_____

❑ *Scientists are looking for life on other planets. How would finding life on another planet change our world?*

WHAT TO EXPECT

For children, the world is full of unknowns and possibilities. They will have seen comics, watched some scientific television programs, and viewed some cartoons that talked about life on other planets. Expect them to become more animated talking about this topic than the adults. They might discuss how we would communicate with aliens, the things they could teach us, or just how different from us they might be.

Keep the Conversation Going by . . .

Asking your child how he feels about the possibility of life on other planets. If scientists discovered a space alien, would he want to meet it? Does he think a space alien would want to meet him? If life on another planet was found, does your child think that he would be able to take a vacation to that planet? What would he pack? Would he be able to buy things that were made by space aliens? Would he be worried about having contact with life from another planet?

316

DATE: _____ / _____ / _____

❑ *What do you think it takes for two people to become good friends?*

WHAT TO EXPECT

Even though it won't be specifically talked about, each child will need to reflect on whether they have the qualities that allow them to be a good friend. Children may say that sharing possessions, doing things together, or having fun together helps two people be good friends. Adults understand that good friendships require much more.

Keep the Conversation Going by . . .

Asking your child to tell you a little bit about her best friend. Who is her best friend? How did they become good friends? What do they have in common? Do these similarities make them closer? Was this person always her best friend? If not, what changed with the person that she had previously been close too? Who does your child think your best friend is? Why does she think you two are good friends?

DATE:_____ /_____ /_____

❏ *If you had a robot, what would you have the robot do for you?*

WHAT TO EXPECT
Everyone in the family will want the robot to do their work. Your children will be excited to imagine a robot making their beds, doing their chores, and making them a snack. They will easily come up with a long list of ways a robot could help them in their daily life. You can chime in with your own list of jobs you would delegate to a robot.

Keep the Conversation Going by . . .
Asking your child to tell you more about the robot. What would she name her robot? Would she take her robot out of the house? What would the robot look like? What color would the robot be? Would the robot be on a remote control? Why would she want the robot to do that particular task? If the robot could do more than one thing, what other things would it be able to do? Take this conversation starter further by asking your child to draw a picture of her robot after dinner has ended.

DATE:_____ /_____ /_____

❑ *What makes someone a good parent?*

WHAT TO EXPECT

Direct this question first to the youngest person at the dinner table and progressively work up the age scale. It is important that you just listen to what your children have to say, and not be defensive or add qualifiers. Children are likely to say a good parent plays outside with their children, lets them have dessert, or allows them to stay up late—all the things your child enjoys and thinks are very special when they happen. When it is your turn to address the conversation starter as the parent, talk about the qualities you saw in your parents as opposed to telling your children how you are trying to be a good parent or what you do as a parent.

Keep the Conversation Going by . . .

Asking your child to put himself in your shoes. What would it be like to be a parent? What are the responsibilities that a parent has? What are some things that might make it hard to be a good parent? Does your child think he would be a good parent? Does he think you are a good parent? What does he think would make someone the best parent ever?

DATE: _____ / _____ / _____

❑ *What makes you different from other people in your classroom?*

WHAT TO EXPECT

Expect your children to reflect on their unique characteristics or qualities. Children will define their differences in terms of physical characteristics. "I have red hair." "I'm tall." Children will focus on the things that strike them as being visually the most different. Adults will define their differences in terms of values, relationship skills, or work styles.

Keep the Conversation Going by . . .

Asking your child if she has thought about this difference before. How does she feel about being different in that way? Is this difference a good thing or a bad thing? Has anyone ever mentioned this difference to her before? What makes her different from the other people in her family? Are those differences good or bad?

DATE: _____ / _____ / _____

❑ *If you were going to write a song, what would it be about?*

WHAT TO EXPECT

Expect your children to need to hear other people answer this conversation starter first to help them better understand the question. That being said, adults will come up with themes that put their life in perspective. Younger members of the family will develop songs that describe where they want to go in life. They might also make up songs about silly things to get a laugh, such as a song about Jell-o up their noses.

Keep the Conversation Going by . . .

Asking your child for details about her song. What genre of music would it be? Country? Rock? Rap? What tune would it be set to? Would it be set to a familiar tune or to something your child came up with by herself? Ask her to sing some of the song for you. The family could suggest lyrics. Or, the whole family could participate in coming up with a song that describes your family.

DATE:_____ /_____ /_____

❑ *What is the best thing about keeping a secret?*

WHAT TO EXPECT

This question will bring forth smiles and giggles as your children think about secrets they have recently held or may still be holding. For children, secrets usually amount to knowing what X is going to give Y for a special occasion like an upcoming birthday. Kids like secrets because it makes them feel in the know or part of a special group, so your child might say keeping a secret makes her feel special. A young child may spill a few secrets in the process, such as who his best friend likes.

Keep the Conversation Going by . . .

Having your child tell you how he feels about keeping secrets. Does he enjoy being in on the secret? Why? Does it make him feel that people trust him? Is he good at keeping secrets? Has he ever told a secret that he was supposed to keep quiet about? What were the consequences? Has he ever kept a secret for a long time? How does he feel about that?

DATE:_____ /_____ /_____

❑ *Tell us about the best TV commercial you have ever seen.*

WHAT TO EXPECT

Almost everyone watches TV, and we all tend to get drawn into commercials. So everyone will have something to say. It will be interesting to see if your child's favorite TV commercial advertises a product that your child uses or is even likely to buy. Your child may choose a commercial he finds particularly funny or attention-getting.

Keep the Conversation Going by . . .

Encouraging your child to tell you more. When did she see that commercial? What about the commercial captured her attention? Was it funny? Sad? If she is old enough, ask her if she has ever bought or would ever consider buying that product. Did the commercial play a role in her answer?

DATE:_____ / _____ / _____

❑ *Which animal has a better life: a monkey in a zoo, a horse on a ranch, or a wild goose?*

WHAT TO EXPECT

Your kids will have to think about what leads to happiness—having your basic needs met, doing meaningful work, or having complete freedom with the accompanying dangers. Children ten and under will likely pick the horse because they see not only the horse, but the richness of living on a big, wide-open ranch. Children between eleven and thirteen may pick the wild goose. A child who has just been to the zoo or is fascinated by monkeys might choose the monkey.

Keep the Conversation Going by . . .

Encouraging your child to tell you why he chose the option he chose. What are the advantages to being that particular animal? What would he like about where each animal lives, eats, or sleeps? What are the disadvantages to being the two animals he did not choose? Are there advantages to being those animals even though he wouldn't want to be them?

DATE:_____ /_____ /_____

❑ *If you could plant your teeth when they fall out, what kind of tree or plant would you like to grow from them?*

WHAT TO EXPECT

Your children may get very imaginative with this question. Their initial response will be to think of trees or plants they are familiar with, such as apple trees or watermelon plants. As the conversation moves along, a child might suggest a money tree, gumball plant, or ice cream tree. Tell your child how old your own tooth trees would be if you had planted them when your teeth fell out.

Keep the Conversation Going by . . .

Asking what it would be like if your child planted a tooth and the tree that came up grew lots of new teeth you could pick. What would he do with all the new teeth he grew? What happens with the teeth he loses now? If he believes in the Tooth Fairy, what does she do with the teeth she collects? Are there other things it would be fun to plant, like quarters, matchbox cars, or Barbie shoes? Has he ever planted a real seed and seen it grow?

DATE: _____ / _____ / _____

❑ *Finish this sentence: "When I get mad, the first thing I do is . . . "*

WHAT TO EXPECT

Many children have difficulty recognizing when they get angry, and their inability to identify those feelings makes it difficult for them to control their outbursts. Children who do a good job controlling their emotions will be able to readily answer this question. They may mention talking to a parent or teacher, looking for solutions to the problem, or screaming but then moving on. Children who tend to have outbursts will have difficulty answering this question; they will need understanding and gentle guidance through the follow-up questions.

Keep the Conversation Going by . . .

Asking your child how she knows when she is getting angry. Does she feel frustrated? Does she feel hot? Does she know she is getting angry before others know it? Has anyone ever pointed her anger out to her before she realized that she was, indeed, angry? Does the first thing she tries often help her get her anger under control? What makes her mad most often?

DATE:_____ /_____ /_____

❑ *Tell us about how you keep yourself orga-*
nized during the day.

WHAT TO EXPECT

Expect your child to examine his or her capacity for
organization, which is a good skill. Your kids will talk
about the routine that is more or less provided for
them, but just understanding that they have a routine is
a good start. Your child will think through all the things
in her routine and may name things like hanging up her
coat, putting her lunchbox away at school, and packing
her backpack to come home. The adolescents and the
adults at the table will candidly discuss their organization skills.

Keep the Conversation Going by . . .

Having your child tell you how organization helps him.
Why is it important that he be organized? Can he recall
a near disaster that happened to him or to someone
else because they weren't organized? In what areas of
his life is it most important to him to be organized? For
example, is it important for him to organize his homework? His toys? His clothes? Is it more important for
him to organize some things instead of others? Have
your child tell you how he can become better organized, then tell him how you keep yourself organized.

DATE:_____ /_____ /_____

❑ *If you were to meet a space alien, what three activities would you do with it?*

WHAT TO EXPECT

This question will let the children dominate the conversation. They will have lots of activities that they will want to try with an alien, such as playing basketball, standing on their heads, playing a game, or digging in the sandbox. They will also probably want to take the alien to school to show all their friends. The idea of engaging with an alien will be enticing.

Keep the Conversation Going by . . .

Asking your child how she thinks the space alien will respond to her. Will it be kind? Will it be scared? How will they communicate with each other? What would her friends at school think if she brought the alien to school? Would the alien be able to do all the things she can do? Are there things the alien could do that she can't?

DATE:_____ /_____ /_____

❑ *If you could live at any time in the past,*
what era would you live in?

WHAT TO EXPECT

Among other things, your children will need to consider what it would be like to live without some of
our modern conveniences. Children are apt to pick a
type of person who lived in a particular time instead of
choosing a specific era. For example, expect them to
say things like, "I want to be a pirate" or "I want to be
a mountain man." The adults at the table may select a
time of considerable change, envisioning themselves as
participants in the developing opportunities.

Keep the Conversation Going by . . .

Helping your child picture what it would have been like
to live during her chosen era (or as her chosen type
of person). Ask her what the most enjoyable or exciting thing about living back then would be. What would
be the most uncomfortable or inconvenient thing that
she would encounter? What does she have now that
she wouldn't have had if she lived back then? Would it
be worth it to give up some modern conveniences to
live back then?

DATE:_____ /_____ /_____

❑ *If we were taking a family portrait and you could dress us any way or have us do anything in it, what would you choose?*

WHAT TO EXPECT

Expect your children to envision a family portrait that is fun in some way. Maybe you're all wearing crowns, sitting on the backs of dolphins, or standing on your heads. They will enjoy the thought of jazzing up a picture because for most kids, taking portraits is boring and tiresome. The focus for them will be the fun you would have taking the photo. For adults, the focus is on the tangible photo that will symbolize your family for years to come.

Keep the Conversation Going by . . .

Having your child tell you why he chose that type of photo. Where would he hang it in the house? Does he think everyone would enjoy taking that kind of photo? What is usually the worst thing about taking portrait photos? Why does he think adults like to have portraits? If he were the photographer, what would he do to get everyone to smile for the camera?

DATE:_____ / _____ / _____

❑ *If you were made king or queen of our country, what laws would you make?*

WHAT TO EXPECT

Your children under age eight will think of laws that would make things fun, like no peas for dinner, roller blades for everyone, or later bedtimes. Older children may be a bit more thoughtful and talk about important laws that govern behavior like no stealing or no hitting. You can talk about how many laws we have in our country and what the purpose of them is and maybe mention some laws you might make.

Keep the Conversation Going by . . .

Asking your child why he would choose those laws. How would he enforce them? Would it be hard to be king or queen and be in charge of everyone in your country? How would he make sure he was a fair king or queen? Why does he think we don't have a king or queen in our country? Would he wear a crown or special robe? Sit on a throne? Live in a palace? What would the citizens think about a leader who did that?

DATE:_____ /_____ /_____

❑ *Would you rather be a tour guide of a city, a national park, or a museum?*

WHAT TO EXPECT

Expect each one of your children to consider the setting that best suits them. Younger family members may respond based upon their experiences, so if your child is awestruck by museums, that will likely be his answer. Children who have had experiences in all three settings may be developing environmental preferences based upon interests and needs and their answers will reflect this.

Keep the Conversation Going by . . .

Asking your child why she chose that location over the other possibilities. Does she have a specific city, park, or museum in mind for the tour? What are some of the things she might point out to others during the tour? Have your child practice her tour guide skills by asking her to give you a tour of one of the rooms in your house after dinner.

DATE: _____ / _____ / _____

❑ *If you invited your favorite cartoon char-acter to dinner, what would happen?*

WHAT TO EXPECT

Your children will revel in describing the chaos that would ensue. Whoever they choose is likely to behave inappropriately and make everyone laugh. Your child may describe how the character eats, what he says, how he acts, and how the family reacts to the situation. There will likely be a lot of activity involved in the description. You can offer your own scenarios with characters you would choose or those you would have chosen as a child.

Keep the Conversation Going by . . .

Asking your child why he chose that particular char-acter. Why does he think the cartoonist created that character? Where does he think he got the idea from? Are there cartoon characters he would not want to invite into your house? Why? What might happen?

DATE:_____ /_____ /_____

❑ *What does the phrase "the life of the party" mean to you?*

WHAT TO EXPECT

Everyone will agree that the life of the party is the center of attention and each child will introspectively examine his or her role at party-like events. Expect your children to think that being the life of the party is always a good thing because they interpret it to mean having fun. They don't have any negative connotations about this in the way adults might. You can share your thoughts about why being the life of the party might not always be the best thing.

Keep the Conversation Going by . . .

Asking your child if she has ever been the life of the party. What were the circumstances? What kind of a party was it? Who was there? How did she end up being the life of the party? What did she do? What are the advantages of being the life of the party? The disadvantages?

DATE:_____ /_____ /_____

❑ *What is one activity that you enjoy now that you hope to enjoy for many years to come?*

WHAT TO EXPECT

This question asks your children to examine the long-term implications of their current activities. The implication of the question is whether their current activities are an investment in their future. Expect your children to name activities that they are now doing a lot. Older members of the family will thoughtfully select one activity that they are likely to continue doing for many years, such as dancing, swimming, or playing tennis.

Keep the Conversation Going by . . .

Asking your child to tell you why he chose that activity. Is it something he's good at? Something he really likes? Can he picture himself doing that activity when he is in high school? College? When he is a senior citizen? Will he get better at that activity as he keeps practicing it? Tell your child about an activity that you have been doing for many years—maybe since you were his age.

DATE:_____ /_____ /_____

❏ *Do you remember what it was like learning to swim?*

WHAT TO EXPECT

Your children will reflect back on when they learned to swim and especially on who taught them to swim. Most children are initially scared to go into deep water, so they will vividly remember that first time when they tried to learn to swim and the feeling of accomplishment when they did it.

Keep the Conversation Going by . . .

Asking your child how she felt when she first learned to swim. Was she scared? Did she feel confident? How does she feel about swimming now? Has she learned what to do? Does she enjoy it? What is her favorite stroke? Would she like to swim more? Does she think swimming is good exercise?

DATE:_____ / _____ / _____

❑ *If you were going to make a float for a parade, what would your float look like?*

WHAT TO EXPECT

Your children will most likely reflect on the types of floats they personally enjoy which might include cartoon characters, actors from favorite TV shows, or lots of moving parts and fun activities. Expect your child to envision a float that would be hard for her to actually construct, with many complicated details. The float will probably express a current interest she has.

Keep the Conversation Going by . . .

Encouraging your child to tell you more about her float. How big would the float be? Would it fit in the back of a pickup truck or would she need a long trailer? What will the float be made out of? Would your child be able to ride on the float? What kind of parade would her float be in?

DATE: _____ / _____ / _____

❑ *Who is your favorite character from a book, a comic, or a movie?*

WHAT TO EXPECT

Expect everyone at your table to have a favorite character. For children six years old and younger, it might be someone like Mary Poppins, Elmo, or a character from a picture book he has recently read. Older children will focus on characters they think are cool or neat or one from a current TV show. Be sure to talk about your favorite character as well.

Keep the Conversation Going by . . .

Asking your child to tell you more about his favorite character. Was this character in a movie, book, or comic? What does your child like about that character? Can he relate to them? Does he think that he is like that character in some ways? Does he wish he was more like that character? In what way? Does your child think he would be a good movie, film, or comic book character? Why? Be sure to tell your child about your favorite character too.

DATE:_____ /_____ /_____

❑ *If you were in charge of building a new community center, what kinds of activities would you put in it for people to do?*

WHAT TO EXPECT

Expect each family member to want to include activities that they personally enjoy in the community center. Your son may want to have a basketball court or an ice hockey arena. Your daughter may want a swimming pool or a dance studio. Dad may want a handball court, and Mom might want fitness equipment. However, the discussion will make every member of the family a little more sensitive to the activities that interest those of other ages and genders.

Keep the Conversation Going by . . .

Encouraging your child to think about what the discussion revealed about other people's interests. Did he learn things about your family that he didn't know before? Would it be likely that the city would have enough money to build a community center large enough for all of the activities your family has mentioned? How would your child go about deciding which activities to include and which ones to set aside?

DATE:_____ /_____ /_____

❑ *Some people insist they have seen UFO's. What do you think they are seeing?*

WHAT TO EXPECT

This question will prompt your children to think about the unexpected. Kids are more likely to embrace the possibility of UFOs than the adults, so they may say they believe they are real flying saucers. When asked about other alternatives, they may think of things like planes, balloons, clouds, or helicopters.

Keep the Conversation Going by . . .

Asking your child where he thinks UFOs come from. Is our military launching them? Do they come from outer space? If so, why does he think they are coming here? Does your child think he'll ever see one? What does he think a UFO would look like? Would it be dangerous to approach one? Would he be afraid to see one? What does he think the inside of a UFO would look like?

DATE:_____ /_____ /_____

❑ *What would you do if you lived next door to someone who didn't mow their grass in the summer, rake their leaves in the fall, or shovel their sidewalk in the winter?*

WHAT TO EXPECT

This conversation starter will give your kids an opportunity to consider what might work and what responses would probably only make matters worse. Some family members will likely suggest a confrontational approach. Others will likely suggest a live-and-let-live approach. Some might suggest helping the neighbor, and others might suggest investigating how to summon the power of city ordinances.

Keep the Conversation Going by . . .

Asking your child why the condition of the neighbor's property would matter to your family. How would it affect her? How does she think the neighbor would respond to her way of dealing with situation? Why might someone let their property get out of control? Are there any reasons your child can think of? What would happen if your family let your property get out of control?

DATE:_____ /_____ /_____

❑ *What would you do if you learned that someone in our community wasn't getting enough to eat or didn't have a dry and warm place to sleep?*

WHAT TO EXPECT

Expect your children to take a moment to consider people less fortunate than themselves. Your kids may need to be told that there are such people in their community. Their first reaction will be to offer personal assistance—take them food or a blanket or maybe invite them into your home. As the conversation flows, they will probably hear adults talking about the dangers of inviting strangers into the home and will work to brainstorm other ideas with you.

Keep the Conversation Going by . . .

Asking your child how he felt when he learned that there are people in his community who struggle like this. Was he surprised? Sad? How would he feel if a close friend or family member was in that situation? Would he try to help? What would he do? Can he think of a way to help people who are dealing with those problems even if he doesn't know who they are?

DATE:_____ /_____ /_____

❑ *How would you like to spend a weekend during the summer: camping, playing on a playground, or playing video games?*

WHAT TO EXPECT

Each of your children will reflect on what they like to do with their leisure time. In general, you can expect them to want to do something that involves playing with other children, even if it is parallel play like playing a video game. Kids who have been to camp and had a good experience might choose that. Adolescents might also pick camping, seeing that as new and different.

Keep the Conversation Going by . . .

Encouraging your child to explain his decision. Why did he choose the option that he chose? Why did he decide to forego the other options? Does he think he'll have more fun doing the option that he chose? When was the last time he did that thing? Who would he want to do it with him? If your child decided he wanted to go camping or wanted to play on a playground, ask him what activities he would want to be involved in. Would he want to try archery or play basketball? If he wants to play video games, ask him what game or games he'd like to try.

DATE:_____ /_____ /_____

❏ *If you found a $20 bill on the street, what would you do?*

WHAT TO EXPECT

This question helps children think through the moral repercussions of finding something that doesn't belong to them. Children under age eight will think only of how they could spend the money. Your older children may consider where the money might have come from. They will think about what their responsibility is to that person and might discuss looking around to see who might have lost it or even taking it to the police.

Keep the Conversation Going by . . .

Asking how your child imagines the money could have gotten there. If he dropped some money on the street, what would he hope would happen if someone else found it? What is the best way to return a lost item to its owner? How might that person feel when he realizes he lost his money?

DATE:_____ /_____ /_____

❑ *Have you ever thought of running away*
from home?

WHAT TO EXPECT

At one point in time or another, nearly all children have
thought of running away from home, if for no other reason than for the excitement of the adventure. Other
children may have considered it as a reaction to being
angry or upset. So expect everyone to have a story to
tell. Your children will learn that you were once a child
who had many of the same thoughts and frustrations
that they have experienced.

Keep the Conversation Going by . . .

Having your child tell you what made him want to run
away from home. Is this something he has thought about
often? Did he actually leave home? If so, have him tell you
about that experience. How far did he go? What did he
bring with him? What made him return home? Is he glad
he returned? If something like this happened again, what
could he do instead of running away?

DATE:_____ /_____ /_____

❑ *What do you think it takes to be a good doctor?*

WHAT TO EXPECT

Your children will think about the skill set that a good doctor should possess and will, at least implicitly, ask themselves whether they have that skill set. Expect your children to think that being smart is the most important skill. The adults will add that it also takes compassion, dedication, and good listening skills to be a really good doctor.

Keep the Conversation Going by . . .

Encouraging your child to tell you more. Does she know a good doctor? Has she ever thought about whether she would like to be a doctor? What does she think about her current doctor? Does she think he or she is good at the job? Why or why not?

DATE:_____ /_____ /_____

❑ *Would you rather be a policeofficer, a firefighter, or a teacher?*

WHAT TO EXPECT

Your children will consider what each job entails and whether they would find it interesting. Children ten years old and younger may pick a firefighter because they have probably seen a fire truck and maybe even had a firefighter visit their school. Children who enjoy school may choose a teacher. Some may pick a policeofficer because of the excitement and danger involved.

Keep the Conversation Going by . . .

Encouraging your child to tell you why she chose the option that she chose. Does she think her chosen option would be fun? Scary? Exciting? Fulfilling? What would be the challenges of each specific job? The rewards? Is this a job that your child might actually want to take on at some point?

DATE:_____ /_____ /_____

❑ *Why do you think people eat together?*

WHAT TO EXPECT

Most children have never thought about this. This question will help your children understand the social connection that food has. Your child may first respond that you eat together because the food is ready and there is enough for everyone. As you talk about this together, you can point out how eating together gives you something to share and time to talk to each other and your child will begin to understand the ways food brings people together.

Keep the Conversation Going by . . .

Asking your child what it would be like if everyone ate their meals separately. Would she find it lonely? Does she think that sharing food teaches people to share other things? When she helps cook something, does she enjoy seeing other people eat and enjoy it? Does sitting around the table together bring your family closer together? How do you feel during family dinners?

DATE:_____ /_____ /_____

❑ *Why is it that when you put socks in the washing machine, you often get one less sock out than you put in? What happens to those missing socks?*

WHAT TO EXPECT

The creative answers to this question will elicit laughter from everyone at the table. The explanations will get increasingly imaginative and creative with each successive storyteller. Your child might talk about a monster that eats socks, about a hiding place the socks go to, or how some socks magically turn themselves into underwear while in the washing machine. This is a good opportunity for some imaginative storytelling.

Keep the Conversation Going by . . .

Asking your child if she is missing any socks right now. Does she think that someplace there is a huge box of missing socks? How do the socks escape from the dryer? Does she think white socks escape more frequently than colored socks or vice versa? Do white socks and colored socks end up at the same place? Has your child ever lost one of her favorite socks? Where does she think that particular sock is now?

DATE:_____ /_____ /_____

❑ *If you were going to mix different flavors of soda together to get one perfect tasting soda, which flavors would you mix?*

WHAT TO EXPECT

Some kids already do this and have perfected the mixture that suits their taste buds. Many others have tried it, but didn't like the result. So expect your children to be excited to share their experiences at this. If your child hasn't done this, she will certainly come up with some interesting flavor combinations. The adults will most likely sit back with puzzled looks on their faces.

Keep the Conversation Going by . . .

Asking your child if he has ever actually mixed those sodas. If so, what combinations did he try before he found one that he liked? If not, how many combinations does he think he would have to try before finding one that works? Does he think your family could patent that flavor and make some serious money? What would he call it? Have any of his friends tried this and found a combination they like? What would happen if your child mixed other types of drinks? Would any of those mix well together?

DATE:_____ /_____ /_____

❑ *If you were going to write a comic book that had an evil villain in the story, what would that villain be like?*

WHAT TO EXPECT

Most children love comic books. Your child may have even thought about making his own variation on a comic book. Being primed for this question, he will have ideas. Although you might not enjoy hearing your child describe evil villains in a glorified way, remember that the purpose of the conversation starter is to let your child's imagination roam. He will likely come up with some very evil details.

Keep the Conversation Going by . . .

Asking your child to tell you more about his villain. What would the villain look like? Why did this person become a villain? Was he or she previously a good guy? What does the villain do that's so bad? Is the villain still alive at the end of the story? Have your child tell you a little more about the story as a whole. What is the setting for the story? Who is the hero? How does your child's hero stop the villain? Does he stop the villain?

DATE:_____ /_____ /_____

❏ *Would you prefer to have an exciting job that doesn't pay much money or a boring job that pays a lot of money?*

WHAT TO EXPECT

For the most part, you can expect children to choose the exciting job that doesn't pay much money. At this age, they aren't as concerned with money and the need to support a family. Excitement is all that matters and they will have a hard time understanding why anyone would want a job they find boring. The majority of older people will choose the boring job that pays a lot of money. Go figure.

Keep the Conversation Going by . . .

Encouraging your child to explain what kinds of jobs she finds exciting. What about those jobs makes them interesting to her? How much money would she have to earn in order to put up with a boring job? Have her tell you what kinds of jobs she finds to be boring. Can she think of any exciting jobs that do pay a lot of money? If so, what are they and would she be interested in working one of them?

DATE:_____ /_____ /_____

❑ *What would it be like to live without running water?*

WHAT TO EXPECT

Expect this conversation starter to help your children gain some appreciation for conveniences that they probably take for granted. Children may have a hard time thinking of all of the ways they use and count on running water, although they will likely think of flushing toilets and taking baths pretty quickly. You will probably have to say, "And we couldn't do this, and we wouldn't have that."

Keep the Conversation Going by . . .

Asking your child if there are any advantages to not having running water. What would it be like to have to go outside to go to the bathroom? Would he like not being able to take a bath? Would the disadvantages outweigh anything that might be fun about it? How would school, church, or going to a friend's house be different? Ask your child if he knows how long ago it was when your family members did not have running water in the house. If he's not sure, tell him.

DATE: _____ / _____ / _____

❏ *Would you rather be a carpenter, a writer, or a chemist?*

WHAT TO EXPECT

You may be surprised if your daughter tells you she wants to be a carpenter, but your children may have answers you would not anticipate for this question. Many children are fascinated by carpentry because it creates such a clear and visual result. Chemistry may sound interesting to kids who are just starting to do some basic experiments, like soaking pennies in vinegar and salt. Being a writer may appeal to your children who enjoy reading or being read to.

Keep the Conversation Going by . . .

Asking your child to tell you what she knows about the profession that she chose. Does she know anyone who does one of these jobs? How much does she think a carpenter makes an hour? A writer? A chemist? How does one become a carpenter, writer, or chemist? Does your child think that she may want to eventually work in this profession? If not, what can she see herself doing?

DATE:_____ /_____ /_____

❑ *What is the grossest thing you have ever smelled?*

WHAT TO EXPECT

Expect this conversation starter to bring laughter and mirth to people of all ages at your dinner table, but it is a topic that is best saved until after dinner so it does not ruin anyone's appetite. The stories will build on each other and some people may pretend to feel sick or completely grossed out by the entire conversation.

Keep the Conversation Going by . . .

Asking your child where she smelled that. What did she do when she caught a whiff of it? Why does she think it smelled like that? As a family, list ten additional things that are stinky (dirty laundry, skunks, and so on). For a twist, let everyone at your table know that his or her answer has to be smellier than the previous answer.

DATE:_____ /_____ /_____

❑ *What three words best describe how you are feeling right now?*

WHAT TO EXPECT

Expect your children to need some time to reflect on their feelings; and to have some difficulty finding the right words to describe those feelings. Everyone will be challenged by this question because most of us don't do a good job of labeling our feelings. Your child might focus on physical feelings such as hungry, tired, or itchy since those are easiest for him to describe. He's not likely to go into emotional depth and will be satisfied with just choosing a simple emotion like happy or bored.

Keep the Conversation Going by . . .

Thanking your child for sharing his feelings and encouraging him to share more. Ask him if the words he used usually describe his feelings or if he has distinctly different feelings tonight compared to most evenings. Why does he think he feels this way tonight? Did something happen during the day that made him feel this way? Does he think he'll feel this way tomorrow too? Be sure to tell your child how you are feeling tonight too.

DATE:_____ /_____ /_____

❑ *What thing have you made yourself that you are really proud of?*

WHAT TO EXPECT

Children of all ages have experience making things. Your child will choose an item she thought was challenging to make (such as a really difficult model kit) or something she thought turned out beautifully (like a birthday card for Mom). If your child has recently learned how to cook or bake, a dish she made might be the answer. Children are often usually proud of things they used their imaginations to create, such as forts or homemade hockey sticks.

Keep the Conversation Going by . . .

Asking your child when she made this. How long did it take her? Does she still have it? If she made it again, how would she do it differently? What else would she like to make? Does she know how to do it or would she like some help doing it? Talk about something your child made for you that you treasure, so she gets some positive feedback on her creations.

DATE:_____ /_____ /_____

❏ *If school lasted one extra hour a day, what subject would you want to be taught?*

WHAT TO EXPECT

Expect your child to choose her favorite subject, such as science, art, or gym. Children over age nine may get creative and come up with subjects that aren't taught in school, but which they wish were, such as scuba diving, hair braiding, or origami. The answers to the question will help you understand what things your child likes about school and what kinds of things she is interested in learning more about.

Keep the Conversation Going by . . .

Encouraging your child to tell you what she would teach if she was asked to fill the last hour of school. Would she really want to go to school for an extra hour a day to learn or do the thing she has named? Would other kids be interested in the same thing she is? Why don't kids get to pick what they learn at school?

DATE: _____ / _____ / _____

❑ *What foods do you eat to help you stay fit and healthy?*

WHAT TO EXPECT

This will begin a discussion about nutrition and healthy eating. Your children are probably very aware of what food is healthy and what is not. One answer a lot of children may offer is milk, since they've been taught it is healthy to drink. They may name vegetables they do eat and fruits that they like.

Keep the Conversation Going by...

Asking your child what foods he eats that might not be so healthy. Why does he eat them if he knows they are not good for his body? What healthy foods are on the dinner table right now? Does he eat healthy foods often enough? If there are healthy foods he does not like, why doesn't he like them? What do healthy foods do for our bodies?

DATE:_____ /_____ /_____

❑ *Imagine that today is a good friend's birthday, but you forgot. You need a present to give him right away. What would you choose from around the house to give him?*

WHAT TO EXPECT

Your children will immediately think of their own possessions that a friend might like, but may be hesitant to want to give up something! Don't be surprised if they choose something the friend might not really like because of this, or if they choose something they personally don't really like. Your child is more likely to want to part with an item if he has duplicates; if he has ten action figures, then giving away one wouldn't be as hard.

Keep the Conversation Going by...

Asking your child if he would tell his friend he forgot about the birthday. What would he say? How would the friend feel? How would he wrap the gift if there was no wrapping paper in the house? Would he use comics? Draw his own wrapping paper? What would he use for a bow?

DATE:_____ / _____ / _____

❑ *You sometimes hear people say, "He's a good person." What do they mean? What makes a good person?*

WHAT TO EXPECT

Expect your children to reflect on the qualities of what they think makes a good person. Children will choose qualities that are important to them, such as doing nice things for other people, sharing, being friendly, or following rules. They are likely to focus on behaviors they have been taught are good, like telling the truth and being polite. Be sure to share your opinion about what makes a good person.

Keep the Conversation Going by . . .

Asking your child who he thinks is a good person. Is there anyone outside of your family that fits into that category? What special qualities does that person have? Does your child think he's a good person? Why? What does he do to put that image across? Is it easy for someone to be a good person or does it take some work? Why is it important to be a good person? Be sure to chime in on this conversation and make sure your child knows what you think makes someone good.

DATE: _____ / _____ / _____

❑ *If you could be a contestant on any game or competition show, which one would you choose?*

WHAT TO EXPECT

Your child will pick a show that he thinks is fun and exciting. His choice may be driven mostly by the activity that happens on the show. Most children won't find quiz shows entertaining and are more likely to enjoy shows where people have to do crazy or silly things or compete in ways that your child would be interested in (such as singing competitions or dance competitions).

Keep the Conversation Going by . . .

Asking your child if she thinks it would be hard to compete on a show. Would it be fun to try something new if there was a chance you could win money or prizes? How would you feel if you went on the show and lost? If our family had to compete on a show, which one would you choose for us? What would it be like if we won?

DATE:_____ / _____ / _____

❑ *Would you rather run a miniature golf course in the Statue of Liberty, be a tow boat operator on the Mississippi River, or build playgrounds in the Sahara Desert?*

WHAT TO EXPECT

Your child may choose the job which appeals to a recent interest, such as miniature golf. If nothing immediately interests her, she will weigh the possibilities for each option. It can be hard to predict what your children will select. Join in the conversation and share your own choice. Then talk about what each job would really be like.

Keep the Conversation Going by . . .

Asking your child what would be fun about the job she chose. Would she get tired of it and want to try something else? What might be hard about the job? How would she overcome the difficulties? Would she expect a lot of people to visit her or need her services?

DATE:_____ /_____ /_____

❏ *What one relative would you like to have come live with us for a month?*

WHAT TO EXPECT

Your children will consider members of the extended family and how they nurture, support, and enjoy each other. You can expect your children to name a favorite grandparent, aunt, uncle, or cousin. You might talk about a relative in need, such as an ailing grandparent or troubled teen who could benefit from some support through a hard time, which will help your child to think about how family helps each other.

Keep the Conversation Going by . . .

Asking your child why she would like to have that person stay with your family. Would it be hard to have another person living in the house? Where would that person sleep? What would his or her schedule be like? Would it be fun to have that person living in the house? Why? How would having that person living at your house change your child's life? Does she know anyone who has a relative living with them? How does she think that is working out for the family?

DATE: _____ / _____ / _____

❏ *If you could choose any sound to be your alarm in the morning, what would you choose?*

WHAT TO EXPECT

Your children will pick sounds that they find pleasant or connected to good things, such as favorite songs, the buzzer going off on the toaster oven when the waffles are done, or the sound of their hamster spinning its wheel. Some children will enjoy choosing silly noises like cows mooing or bubble gum popping. The conversation will help you understand what kinds of noises have happy connections for your kids. Be sure to offer your own opinion.

Keep the Conversation Going by...

Asking your child if that sound would be loud enough to wake him up. Would he wake up happier if that was the sound he awoke to each day? What sound wakes him up now? Does the way he wakes up affect how he feels that day? Is it hard to wake up some mornings? Does an annoying alarm noise ruin his morning? What could he do to make waking up easier and happier?

365

DATE:_____ /_____ /_____

❑ *Which do you like the most—starting out on a long trip or coming home from a long trip?*

WHAT TO EXPECT

Expect everyone to think about the anticipatory excitement of trips, but to also reflect on the solace that comes from being home again and back in their own space. Children are apt to like the idea of starting a long trip because it appeals to their adventuresome nature and they can easily recall the excitement involved in getting ready to leave. The adults are likely to think back on long trips, and recall that trips were enjoyable, but they were also draining. They will recall the relief they felt in getting back home.

Keep the Conversation Going by . . .

Having your child think about a trip your family has taken. Did he like starting out or coming home best for that trip? Why? Are both options equally enjoyable? Why does he like the start of a trip? What is nice about coming home? Is there anything bad about starting a trip? Is there anything bad about coming home? Did these factors help him decide on his answer?

ABOUT THE AUTHORS

Emily Hall is a fourth-year medical student. She was the guiding force for this book and worked on the project with her parents, **Philip S. Hall, PhD**, and **Nancy D. Hall, EdD**. Philip is a certified psychologist with more than forty years of experience working with children. Nancy works in educational administration and has been a teacher and a school principal, and is currently a dean of a college of education. Together, they have written two books, *Parenting a Defiant Child* and *Educating Oppositional and Defiant Children*, which earned the Golden Lamp Award, the highest honor in educational publishing.